Public Speaking
& Presentations
FOR
DUMMIES

by Malcolm Kushner and Rob Yeung

BICENTENNIAL
1807
WILEY
2007
BICENTENNIAL

John Wiley & Sons, Ltd

Public Speaking & Presentations For Dummies®

Published by
John Wiley & Sons, Ltd
The Atrium
Southern Gate
Chichester
West Sussex
PO19 8SQ
England

E-mail (for orders and customer service enquires): cs-books@wiley.co.uk

Visit our Home Page on www.wiley.com

Copyright © 2007 John Wiley & Sons, Ltd, Chichester, West Sussex, England

Published by John Wiley & Sons, Ltd, Chichester, West Sussex

All Rights Reserved. No part of this publication may be reproduced, stored in a retrieval system or transmitted in any form or by any means, electronic, mechanical, photocopying, recording, scanning or otherwise, except under the terms of the Copyright, Designs and Patents Act 1988 or under the terms of a licence issued by the Copyright Licensing Agency Ltd, 90 Tottenham Court Road, London, W1T 4LP, UK, without the permission in writing of the Publisher. Requests to the Publisher for permission should be addressed to the Permissions Department, John Wiley & Sons, Ltd, The Atrium, Southern Gate, Chichester, West Sussex, PO19 8SQ, England, or emailed to permreq@wiley.co.uk, or faxed to (44) 1243 770620.

Trademarks: Wiley, the Wiley Publishing logo, For Dummies, the Dummies Man logo, A Reference for the Rest of Us!, The Dummies Way, Dummies Daily, The Fun and Easy Way, Dummies.com and related trade dress are trademarks or registered trademarks of John Wiley & Sons, Inc. and/or its affiliates in the United States and other countries, and may not be used without written permission. All other trademarks are the property of their respective owners. Wiley Publishing, Inc., is not associated with any product or vendor mentioned in this book.

LIMIT OF LIABILITY/DISCLAIMER OF WARRANTY: THE PUBLISHER, THE AUTHOR, AND ANYONE ELSE INVOLVED IN PREPARING THIS WORK MAKE NO REPRESENTATIONS OR WARRANTIES WITH RESPECT TO THE ACCURACY OR COMPLETENESS OF THE CONTENTS OF THIS WORK AND SPECIFICALLY DISCLAIM ALL WARRANTIES, INCLUDING WITHOUT LIMITATION WARRANTIES OF FITNESS FOR A PARTICULAR PURPOSE. NO WARRANTY MAY BE CREATED OR EXTENDED BY SALES OR PROMOTIONAL MATERIALS. THE ADVICE AND STRATEGIES CONTAINED HEREIN MAY NOT BE SUITABLE FOR EVERY SITUATION. THIS WORK IS SOLD WITH THE UNDERSTANDING THAT THE PUBLISHER IS NOT ENGAGED IN RENDERING LEGAL, ACCOUNTING, OR OTHER PROFESSIONAL SERVICES. IF PROFESSIONAL ASSISTANCE IS REQUIRED, THE SERVICES OF A COMPETENT PROFESSIONAL PERSON SHOULD BE SOUGHT. NEITHER THE PUBLISHER NOR THE AUTHOR SHALL BE LIABLE FOR DAMAGES ARISING HEREFROM. THE FACT THAT AN ORGANIZATION OR WEBSITE IS REFERRED TO IN THIS WORK AS A CITATION AND/OR A POTENTIAL SOURCE OF FURTHER INFORMATION DOES NOT MEAN THAT THE AUTHOR OR THE PUBLISHER ENDORSES THE INFORMATION THE ORGANIZATION OR WEBSITE MAY PROVIDE OR RECOMMENDATIONS IT MAY MAKE. FURTHER, READERS SHOULD BE AWARE THAT INTERNET WEBSITES LISTED IN THIS WORK MAY HAVE CHANGED OR DISAPPEARED BETWEEN WHEN THIS WORK WAS WRITTEN AND WHEN IT IS READ.

For general information on our other products and services, please contact our Customer Care Department within the U.S. at 800-762-2974, outside the U.S. at 317-572-3993, or fax 317-572-4002.

For technical support, please visit www.wiley.com/techsupport.

Wiley also publishes its books in a variety of electronic formats. Some content that appears in print may not be available in electronic books.

British Library Cataloguing in Publication Data: A catalogue record for this book is available from the British Library

ISBN-13: 978-0-470-03472-9 (PB)

Printed and bound in Great Britain by TJ International Ltd, Padstow, Cornwall.

10 9 8 7 6 5 4 3 2

WILEY

About the Authors

Malcolm Kushner, 'America's Favourite Humour Consultant', is an internationally acclaimed expert on humour and communication and a professional speaker. Since 1982, he has trained thousands of managers, executives, and professionals how to gain a competitive edge with humour. His clients include IBM, Hewlett-Packard, AT&T, Chevron, Aetna, Motorola, and Bank of America.

A popular speaker, his Leading With Laughter presentation features rare video clips of US presidents using humour intentionally and successfully. He has performed the speech at many corporate and association meetings, as well as at the Smithsonian Institute.

A Phi Beta Kappa graduate of the University of Buffalo, Kushner holds a BA in Speech-Communication. His MA in Speech-Communication is from the University of Southern California, where he taught freshman speech. He also has a JD from the University of California Hastings College of the Law. Prior to becoming a humour consultant, he practiced law with a major San Francisco law firm.

Kushner is the author of *The Light Touch: How to Use Humor for Business Success* and *Vintage Humor for Wine Lovers.* He is also a co-creator of the humour exhibit at the Ronald Reagan Presidential Library.

Frequently interviewed by the media, Kushner has been profiled in *Time, USA Today, The New York Times,* and numerous other publications. His television and radio appearances include CNN, National Public Radio, CNBC, *Voice of America,* and *The Larry King Show.* His annual 'Cost of Laughing Index' has been featured on *The Tonight Show* and the front page of *The Wall Street Journal.*

Need a great speaker for your next meeting or event? Contact Malcolm at P.O. Box 7509, Santa Cruz, CA 95061, call 001-831-425-4839, or e-mail him at mk@kushnergroup.com. Visit his Web site at www.kushnergroup.com.

Dr Rob Yeung is a director at business psychology consultancy Talentspace. He is often asked to coach teams and individuals on presentation skills – in particular on developing their presence and charisma when presenting. He travels extensively around the world, running workshops, participating in panel discussions, and giving presentations to audiences of up to many hundreds of people at a time.

He has written for *Guardian, Daily Telegraph,* and *Financial Times* and contributed to publications ranging from *Men's Health* and *New Woman* to *Accountancy* and *Sunday Times*. He has published twelve other books on career and management topics including, in 2006, *The Rules of Office Politics* and *The Rules of EQ* (Cyan/Marshall Cavendish) and *Answering Tough Interview Questions For Dummies* (Wiley).

He is often seen on television including CNN and Channel 4's *Big Brother's Little Brother*. He is also the presenter of the highly acclaimed BBC television series *How to Get Your Dream Job*. A chartered psychologist of the British Psychological Society with a Ph.D. in psychology from the University of London, he has also lectured at a number of business schools and universities.

Need one of the UK's leading psychologists to work with you, your team or your organisation? Drop Dr Rob an email at rob@talentspace.co.uk or visit `www.talentspace.co.uk`.

Malcolm's Dedication

This book is dedicated to my parents – Pauline, Hank, and Helen. Thank you for all of your love and support.

Rob's Dedication

To my parents for their support and unwavering confidence in me. Thanks also to the Talentspace team – especially Steve, Ian, and Penny for keeping the noise down when I was trying to concentrate!

Malcolm's Acknowledgements

Let's start with the people at Wiley. My thanks go to Marc Mikulich, Kathy Cox, and Jennifer Connolly.

Speaking of special thanks, I must shower praise upon my wife Christine Griger who looked at the pages as they came out of the printer. (Jennifer, if you think your job was tough enough, you should have seen what the stuff looked like before Chris's corrections!) And I must thank my son Sam for his encouragement.

Special thanks go to the late San Francisco comedy coach John Cantu. He was a good friend and teacher. And he is greatly missed by everyone who knew him. Loyd Auerbach, Allatia Harris, and N.R. Mitgang also received repeated calls to tap their expertise – and came through every time.

I also want to thank all the other people who were interviewed for this book. They include John Austin, Neil Baron, Donna Bedford, J.E. Aeliot Boswell, Rachael Brune, Joe DiNucci, Steve Fraticelli, James Harris III, Barbara Howard, Joyce Lekas, Marcia Lemmons, Jim Luckaszewski, Chuck McCann, Jeff Raleigh, Steve Resnick, Jackie Roach, Zack Russ, David Schmidt, Ken Sereno, Allen Weiner, Bill Zachmeier, Patty White, Russell Feingold, David Bartlett, Scott Fivash, Kare Anderson, Shawn Whalen, Rich Johnson, and Martin Gonzales Bravo.

Thanks for support and encouragement go to Rich Herzfeld, Bob Reed, Jack Burkett, Stu Silverstein, Linda Mead, Debra DeCuir, Karen Kushner, Barbara Nash, Corwin and Tyler Sparks, and Arthur, Karen, Heather and Amy Tamarkin. Special thanks go to Tom Daly IV at Vital Speeches for granting permission to use so many of the quotes contained in this book.

Rob's Acknowledgements

Thanks again to Jason Dunne at Wiley for offering me the opportunity to work on yet another Dummies book – this time with Malcolm Kushner. Thanks also to my long-suffering editor Daniel Mersey for his tireless enthusiasm and gentle guidance.

Thanks also to my many clients, who have given me the opportunity to practise and hone my presentation and public speaking skills. I remember being so frightened of speaking in front of my classmates at school that I felt physically sick. Nowadays I get pretty much the biggest buzz in my work from standing up in front of an audience and engaging, educating and entertaining them. So thanks to you all.

Publisher's Acknowledgements

We're proud of this book; please send us your comments through our Dummies online registration form located at www.dummies.com/register/.

Some of the people who helped bring this book to market include the following:

Acquisitions, Editorial, and Media Development

Project Editor: Daniel Mersey

Content Editor: Steve Edwards

Executive Editor: Jason Dunne

Copy Editor: Kate O'Leary

Executive Project Editor: Martin Tribe

Cover Photos: © Jupiter Images

Cartoons: Ed McLachlan

Special Help: Jennifer Bingham

Composition Services

Project Coordinator: Jennifer Theriot

Layout and Graphics: Claudia Bell, Carl Byers, Lavonne Cook, Denny Hager, Barry Offringa, Alicia South

Proofreader: Brian H. Walls

Indexer: Techbooks

Publishing and Editorial for Consumer Dummies

    Diane Graves Steele, Vice President and Publisher, Consumer Dummies

    Joyce Pepple, Acquisitions Director, Consumer Dummies

    Kristin A. Cocks, Product Development Director, Consumer Dummies

    Michael Spring, Vice President and Publisher, Travel

    Kelly Regan, Editorial Director, Travel

Publishing for Technology Dummies

    Andy Cummings, Vice President and Publisher, Dummies Technology/General User

Composition Services

    Gerry Fahey, Vice President of Production Services

    Debbie Stailey, Director of Composition Services

Contents at a Glance

Table of Contents

Introduction

● ●

*W*elcome to *Public Speaking & Presentations For Dummies,* a book that we intend to help you have audiences eating out of the palms of your hands. We show you how to use basic speaking skills to influence your boss, colleagues, customers, relatives, loved ones, butcher, baker, candlestick maker, and anyone else who matters in your life.

This book provides all the tools you need to master giving presentations and speaking in public. And that doesn't mean just formal presentations. Some of the most important presentations you ever give may not involve a microphone or a podium, like an impromptu talk about your strategy to some customers; an answer that defuses a hostile question at a business meeting; an impassioned plea to a parking attendant not to issue the ticket. Success or failure in all of these situations, as well as in formal speeches, depends on how you present yourself.

This book covers the full range of skills needed for presenting and public speaking. You can read everything from how to develop and deliver a good presentation to how to think on your feet. An old philosopher once said, 'Every time you open your mouth, your mind is on parade.' This book ensures that your parade looks sharp, sounds smart, and dazzles your audience.

Why You Need This Book

Whether you're dealing with one person or one thousand, the ability to transmit ideas in a coherent and compelling fashion is one of the most important skills you can ever develop. Communicating ideas is a basic survival skill, and it always has been. From the earliest days when we learned to speak as a species and a caveman yelled 'Fire!', people have made speeches to motivate, persuade, and influence each other.

Want to get a good job? Want to get promoted? Want to command the respect of your peers? Want to get a date? The key to success is what you say. To get what you want in life, you have to present yourself forcefully, credibly, and convincingly. Yes, you can speak softly and carry a big stick, but the real winner is the person who talks you out of the stick.

In the information age, public speaking skills are more important than ever before. We live in a society of sound bites. Communication is the currency of the realm. In survey after survey, presentation skills are cited as a key factor in hiring and promotion decisions. The days when you could rise to the top just by being good at your job are over. Boards of directors, executive committees, and customers want more. You have to know how to get your message across.

Now let's admit it. Many people get nervous about giving speeches, particularly in a formal setting. Our goal in writing this book is to rid you of those fears forever. If you simply apply the techniques described in *Public Speaking & Presentations For Dummies,* you'll be able to give a talk more competently than many Oscar-winning performers. We're not saying you'll be the next Prime Minister, but you will see how to deliver a speech in an organised and engaging manner.

And don't fall for the big myth that you have to be 'a born speaker'. Nothing could be further from the truth. Some of the greatest orators in history were anything but 'naturals'. Demosthenes – the famous speaker of ancient Greece – was a shy, stammering introvert when he decided to become a successful orator. He taught himself to speak by rehearsing with rocks in his mouth. If all you have in your mouth is your foot, then you're way ahead of the game.

If you already have the gift of the gab, you can still pick up many tips and tricks from *Public Speaking & Presentations For Dummies.* For example, you wouldn't believe how often experienced speakers completely undermine their entire speech with poorly designed slides and overheads. If you read nothing more than the chapter on how to correct this common mistake (Chapter 10, by the way), this book is well worth your investment.

Let's talk straight. Lots of books exist about public speaking, and they're written by people who have various credentials.

But between the two of us authors, we've taught at universities across the UK and the University of Southern California, worked internationally, ghost-written speeches for leading business executives, travelled the lecture circuit as keynote speakers at major corporate and association meetings, appeared on television in the UK and the US.

We've done all that stuff and more, and that experience is what makes this book unique. It contains a treasure trove of nuts-and-bolts information based on real-life experience. You see what really works and what doesn't. Because if there are mistakes to be made, we've already made them – and now you don't have to repeat them.

About This Book

If you want to improve the full range of your public speaking skills, then read the entire book. You will become an expert communicator.

Too busy to read a whole book? Don't worry. *Public Speaking & Presentations For Dummies* is designed with your time constraints in mind. The book is divided into easy-to-read segments that cover very specific topics. Choose an area of interest, such as dealing with hecklers, and turn directly to it.

Want to know about speaking in different cultures? Well, Chapter 17 is the one for you. If you want more than a dozen different ways to kick off your presentation, see Chapter 6.

Conventions Used in This Book

So you can navigate through this book better, we use the following conventions:

- ✔ *Italic* is used for emphasis and to highlight new words or terms that are defined.
- ✔ **Boldfaced** text is used to indicate keywords in bulleted lists.
- ✔ Monofont is used for Web addresses.

⊯ Sidebars, which are shaded grey boxes with text enclosed in them, consist of information that is interesting to know but not necessarily critical to your understanding of the chapter or section's topic.

Foolish Assumptions

While writing this book, we've made some assumptions about you and your knowledge of public speaking:

⊯ You may be fretting about your next speaking engagement because you don't understand how to engage the audience.

⊯ You may know nothing about giving presentations or public speaking but would like to be prepared in case you're ever asked to speak – impromptu or otherwise.

⊯ You may know quite a bit about public speaking and have a lot of experience, but want to polish your speech development and delivery skills.

⊯ You may know how to give a formal speech but would like to improve your speaking skills in special situations – question-and-answer sessions, panels, roundtables, or debates.

⊯ You may know quite a lot about presenting and public speaking but you want to learn some advanced techniques like using humour successfully or adapting your style for different audiences.

⊯ You may know that no reason exists to fear public speaking, but you fear it anyway and you want to know how to overcome your anxiety.

How This Book Is Organised

Public Speaking & Presentations For Dummies has six major parts, each of which is divided into chapters covering specific topics. The chapters are self-contained units of brilliant insight, so you don't have to plough through them in sequence. You can read chapters separately or together in any order you wish. Don't worry about missing any gems of wisdom. The book is thoroughly cross-referenced and guides you to related items of information.

Each part covers a major area of presenting and public speaking skills. The following is a brief tour of what you can find.

Part I: Getting Started

You've been asked to give a presentation, now what? How do you decide what to talk about? What if you've been given a topic you don't like? Can you change it? How do you find out detailed information about your audience? Where can you get interesting material for your talk? These are some of the questions that we address in this section. Discover how to get your presentation research off to a fast, productive start.

Part II: Preparing Your Presentation or Speech

In today's fast-paced, competitive environment, fortunes can rise or fall on the basis of a single presentation. So your talk had better be good – informative, to the point, attention grabbing, and memorable. And your speech doesn't get that way by luck or accident. Careful preparation – from topic selection to outline structure to choice of material to writing the actual speech – is the key. In this section, we show you how to develop a speech that commands an audience's attention, influences their thinking, and achieves your goals.

Part III: Making Your Presentation or Speech Sparkle

Powerful public speakers are not that different from run-of-the-mill speakers. Both use words. Both use visual aids. And both stand in front of an audience. But really good speakers use really good words. They polish their presentation until it's a gem. They also make sure that their visual aids communicate rather than confound. And when they stand in front of an audience, they appear confident and in control. This part of the book tells you how to give your presentation or speech that 'extra something' that transforms it into an exciting event.

Part IV: Delivering Your Presentation or Speech

When giving a presentation or speech, you need to think about more than just your topic. You have to make decisions about whether you should use a podium; what you should wear; what gestures you should use; how fast you should speak; how you should handle the audience and their questions. And these are just a few of the issues involved in transforming your written message into a masterful oral performance. In this section, we show you how to deliver a presentation that wows your audience. Simple, proven techniques guarantee your success. If you're nervous, shy, or disorganised, don't worry. We also explain how to handle any fears you have about giving presentations or public speaking.

Part V: Common Speaking Situations

Even if you're not a professional speaker, the odds are that you'll have to give a presentation or speech every so often. You may have to address a group of businesspeople from another country. Or you may serve as a panelist at an event sponsored by your club, association, or religious organisation. And in this age of technology and globalism, this part is essential to discover how to speak internationally. In this section, we address these types of common speaking situations, and show you how to anticipate and prepare for them. You even discover how to give a speech 'off the top of your head'.

Part VI: The Part of Tens

In this part, you can find simple types of humour that anyone can use to polish off a presentation or speech. We give you a list of things to check before you speak so you don't leave out any of those important details that can stunt the effectiveness of your talk. And we finish with some top tips for dealing with any stress or anxiety you may feel at having to present to an audience.

Icons Used in This Book

We've included some navigational aids to highlight key points of text for you:

This icon signals important advice about how to maximise the effectiveness of your speech or presentation.

An elephant never forgets, but people do. This icon alerts you to information you'll definitely want to remember.

This icon points to information that justifies your purchase of this book – brilliant advice that you can't readily find any-where else. Most of the information's based on the personal experience, knowledge, and insights that we have collected over the years.

To indicate potential problems, we use this icon.

Where Do I Go from Here?

You hold in your hands a powerful tool – a guide to increasing your influence through the sheer force of your presentations. This tool can be used for good or evil. The choice is up to you. Consider yourself warned. You're now ready to dive into this book. To begin your journey, turn to the Table of Contents or Index, pick a topic of interest, and turn to the page indicated. Good luck in your travels!

Part I
Getting Started

'Someone's broken into my car in the car park and stolen my notes for tonight's speech.'

In this part . . .

The toughest part of preparing a presentation or speech, or doing anything, is getting started. In these chapters, we show you how to take the first steps toward doing what has to be done. You can also find out what information you need to know about your audience to craft a successful presentation. We even cover how to get started researching what you're going to say.

Chapter 1

Giving a Presentation or Speech

*W*hether you're giving your first presentation or your five hundredth, this book can show you how to improve your presentation and public speaking skills. The book is crammed full of practical ideas, techniques, and suggestions; beginners can benefit just from discovering and avoiding basic mistakes, and experienced presenters may appreciate the expert tips and techniques sprinkled throughout these pages. You don't need to read this book from cover to cover (of course, you can if you want to). You can skip chapters and even sections within chapters, focusing only on the material that suits your needs. So if you're looking for an idea of where to start or an idea of what chapters may benefit you the most, just check out the sections that follow to find out what each chapter has to offer.

Finding Out What You Need to Know

Before you give your presentation, or even write it, you need to know a lot of basic information. Chapters 2 and 3 tell you how to get started researching the basics.

Getting down the preliminaries

Getting asked to speak begins the process of making a lot of decisions. The first decision is exactly what to talk about. Even when you're assigned a topic, you generally still have room to shape it. How you decide on an angle depends on the audience – not just their age and gender, but also their education, attitudes, and much more. Chapter 2 tells you what you need to know and how to find it out.

Doing research

No matter what you're talking about, you can improve your speech by doing a little research. We don't mean just locating facts and statistics. You can also find quotes, jokes, and stories to add colour to your speech or presentation. Chapter 3 puts a wealth of research tools and techniques at your disposal, such as using both local and specialist library resources, searching Web sites, and getting other people to do your research for you – for free.

Organising your presentation

After you've got a topic and you've done some research, you need to get organised. To make your presentation flow, you can choose from several patterns: Problem and solution; past, present, and future; and cause and effect. Chapter 4 gives you lots of ideas for ways to organise your material and shows you how to create a useful presentation outline that conforms to your time limits.

Developing Your Presentation

Speaking in front of others scares a lot of people. Many people see writing a speech as a hassle. And doing it right can take a lot of time. But calm down. This part of the book shows you everything you need to know to write a speech or presentation quickly and effectively.

Selecting the right material

You've done research and you've got an outline. Now you need to put some meat on those bones. (Or leaves on those branches if you're a vegetarian.) If you're looking for the key to captivating an audience with statistics, quotes, stories, and examples, you're in luck. We unlock all kinds of potential presentation material in Chapter 5.

Starting and ending your speech

Many people believe that you have to open with a joke, but asking a rhetorical question or using a quotation for the opening – or the conclusion – can involve the audience better. In Chapters 6 and 7, we discuss interesting ways to open and close your presentation, and we give you great ideas to make sure you and your audience reach your conclusion at the same time.

Polishing It Off

Anyone can throw a presentation together, but you also need to make it memorable. If you need to find just that right turn of phrase, develop the winning argument, come up with the perfect example or anecdote that an audience will never forget, or get ideas on how to deliver your speech flawlessly even if you're nervous, Chapters 8 to 10 make polishing your speech and delivery much easier.

Making sure your presentation makes sense

Obviously, your presentation makes perfect sense to you, but the test is whether it makes sense to your audience. If you'd rather not find out that crucial fact as you deliver it, visit Chapter 8 for ideas on how to put a little spit and polish on your presentation to make it stand out from the crowd.

Adding some style

You don't have to be a poet or literary type to put a little richness into your presentation. Certain words and phrases can make more powerful statements than others – and you just have to pick the right ones. Chapter 9 shows you how to use rhetorical techniques to create some colourful lines and phrases to spice up your presentation.

Using visual aids

A picture can paint a thousand words – so see Chapter 10 for everything you need to know to make your graphics look good and to avoid common mistakes. From PowerPoint to overheads to good old-fashioned flipcharts, you can find several great choices for displaying information during your speech or presentation.

Delivering a Presentation

After you've created a brilliant, witty speech or presentation that captures your message exactly, you still have to perform it in front of an audience. So, if your goal is to receive a standing ovation, Chapters 11 to 14 may give you a chance for one.

Overcoming stage fright

If you've gone to all the trouble to create a brilliant presentation, you don't want to ruin it by letting your nerves show up on the podium. If you need to calm your nerves at the outset or find some stress-busting techniques used by professional speakers, check out Chapter 11.

Talking with your body

The way you move and make eye contact affects how your audience receives your message. To ensure that your verbal and non-verbal messages match, check out Chapter 12 and find out all the details on how to move, dress, make eye contact, deal with your hands and habits, and get your other body-language questions answered.

Taking questions

Answering audience questions is an art in itself. What do you do if you don't know the answer? How do you respond to hostile questions? What if the questioners have no idea what they're talking about? Chapter 13 addresses all these issues and shows you how to anticipate questions, design perfect answers, and get an audience to ask questions.

Handling the audience

Your presentation is fantastic but your audience is not: They're heckling you; they're falling asleep; they're leaving! Understanding how to read an audience is an essential skill for anyone who has to speak in public. You have to adapt quickly and know what you're adapting to. To discover how to deal with tough audiences, keep their attention, and get them involved, see Chapter 14.

Preparing for Special Speaking Situations

Giving informal speeches, introducing other speakers, engaging in panel discussions, and handling international audiences are all common speaking situations, but they don't fit into the normal pattern of presenting at a conference or speaking at a meeting. Special meetings require special preparation, and Chapters 15 to 17 show you how to handle all these situations.

Speaking on the spot

Being asked to get up and say a few words about something off-the-cuff is one of the most common, yet dreaded, speaking situations. The good news is that you won't have to spend a lot of time preparing your speech. Of course, that's also the bad news. Chapter 15 tells you how to anticipate those situations, plan for them, and give fabulous impromptu speeches.

Introducing other speakers

If you have to introduce a speaker at a meeting, conference, or convention, you probably wonder how big a deal to make of it. Should the introduction be long and flowery, be just a recitation of the speaker's resume, or involve a lot of research to find some 'inside' stories about the speaker? Find out how to handle your next introduction in Chapter 15.

Speaking on panels or roundtables

Some people think serving on a panel or roundtable is easy. They think they can just wing it because the other panelists can always pick up the slack. If you happen to be more of a slacker than a pick-up-the-slacker, just remember that the audience is going to *compare* you to those other panelists, so you'd better be good. Chapter 16 shows you how to stand out from the crowd when you're speaking on a panel or roundtable.

Speaking at international meetings

Today's global economy has increased the number of businesspeople who speak before international audiences. While language differences are a big challenge, cultural differences can be even bigger. Use Chapter 17 to prepare for your next international meeting so you can avoid embarrassing gaffes.

The Part of Tens

In this section, we show you how to make your presentation sparkle with humour – even if you can't tell a joke. The techniques are so simple that you'll wonder why you didn't use them before. We also point out what to check just before you speak and how to overcome last-minute nerves and the fear factor.

Chapter 2

Getting Ready to Present

● ●

In This Chapter

▶ Preparing for your presentation

▶ Understanding your audience

▶ Connecting with your audience

● ●

*G*etting started is always the toughest part of any activity, including writing a speech or presentation – especially if you don't want to give one in the first place. But don't worry. Speechwriting doesn't have to be torture and can even be fun – well, at least more fun than getting poked in the eye with a sharp stick.

This chapter shows you several simple techniques for getting started with your speech or presentation.

Making Important Preparations

Giving a speech or presentation doesn't start when you step in front of an audience. Giving a talk doesn't even start when you begin writing it. The entire process begins before you even accept the invitation to speak or present. The sections that follow discuss issues you should consider before you even commit yourself to a speaking engagement and things to think about prior to writing the content of your speech or presentation.

Deciding whether you should speak

Just because you're asked to speak doesn't mean you have to. Of course, if your boss asks you to give a talk, you'd better do it, but we're referring to voluntary situations. Unfortunately, most people give little, if any, thought to whether they want to or should speak. Before you accept your next invitation to speak, consider the following issues so you can make the right decision:

- ✔ **Whether you have the time in your diary.** Remember, just because you're asked to speak for 30 minutes doesn't mean that's all the time it takes. You have to get to the event and back, of course, but you also need to leave time to answer questions and be available after you're finished (see Chapter 13 for more information on being available after your talk). And you may need to engage in a bit of chit-chat either before or after your talk with the hosts who invited you. So, a 30-minute presentation can easily take up half of your day.

- ✔ **Whether you have the time to prepare.** Make sure that you have enough time to prepare a presentation that you're proud of and that meets the expectations of your audience – you want to create a great impression. While having an exact formula to follow would be great, in reality, preparing a 30-minute presentation can take hours, days, weeks, or months depending on whom you're speaking to and how important the presentation is. For example, if you need to put together a slide presentation, that could take hours to write. And then, of course, you may need to practise the presentation until you feel comfortable with it. You're the only one who can decide how much time is necessary for preparing your talk.

- ✔ **Whether you have something to say.** Just because someone asks you to present doesn't mean you have anything to say. Sometimes your best talk will be the one you don't give.

- ✔ **Whether to accept immediately.** You don't have to decide the moment someone asks you and you probably shouldn't. Take your time. Sleep on it. Get back to the person after you've had time to think about the considerations above.

Although we're sure you are a great speaker, bear in mind that some people resort to all forms of flattery just to get you to accept their invitation, especially if they're desperate to fill a speaking slot. Don't be swept away by their praise. Even if you truly are the perfect person for their engagement, it may not be something you want to or can do. Politely declining is okay if, after you've considered all the issues, you've concluded that this speaking engagement is not for you.

Figuring out why you're speaking

Three types of speaker exist: Those who make things happen, those who watch things happen, and those who wonder what happened.

To avoid wondering what happened, you should definitely find out why you're speaking in the first place. Here are two effective ways to discover why you're giving a talk:

- ✔ **Figure out the goals of your talk.** Are you trying to inform, persuade, inspire, or entertain?

- ✔ **Examine your motivation for speaking and the audience's motivation for listening.** Have you been asked to speak? Have you been ordered to speak? Do you want to speak? Does the audience want to hear you? Have they been forced to hear you? Will they listen to you?

However you analyse your goals and motivation, the purpose remains the same – to know why you're speaking so you don't end up wondering what happened after it all goes horribly wrong.

Setting specific goals

Most people either set no goals when they decide to give a presentation or set goals that are vague, such as wanting to be a hit, wanting to impress a co-worker or management, or wanting to get the talk over with. However, deciding what you hope to accomplish through speaking – your goals – makes developing yourpresentation easier.

Some examples of goals you may have are

✔ Wanting to build your credibility

✔ Wanting to get the audience to agree with your position

✔ Wanting to make the audience understand something

✔ Wanting to make the audience laugh

Write out your goals before you write your presentation. Then you can easily decide what material to include and exclude. Anything that doesn't further your goals o should be excluded.

Getting the essential information

No matter what type of presentation you've been invited to deliver, certain information is basic and essential. You must first know the name of your contact person. Armed with that knowledge, you can ask your contact to provide the rest of the information that you need. The following lists show some of the questions you want answered.

Ask these questions about the event so you'll know the tone of the meeting and what will be expected from you:

✔ What's the purpose of the meeting?

✔ Is it a regularly scheduled meeting or a special event?

✔ Is it a formal or informal event?

✔ What's the atmosphere – very serious or light?

✔ Will your talk be the main attraction?

Ask these questions about the format to make sure your presentation content is the right length and style to fit properly into the meeting:

✔ What's the agenda for the day?

✔ What should the format be for your presentation:

• A general session?

• A breakout session?

• A panel discussion?

• Before, during, or after a meal?

✔ What time will you begin speaking?

✔ How long will you be expected to speak for?

✔ Will there be other speakers?

✔ When will they be speaking?

✔ What will they be speaking about?

✔ Will any of them be speaking in opposition to your views?

✔ What occurs before your presentation?

✔ What occurs after your presentation?

Ask these questions about the location to make sure that everything you need is available and arranged the way you prefer:

✔ Where will you speak?

- Inside or outside?

- What type of room: banquet, meeting, auditorium, and so on?

✔ How will the room and seating be set up?

✔ What audio/visual and sound equipment will be available for you?

✔ Will there be a podium/table/platform?

Ask these questions about the audience to get an idea of the mood they'll be in when you speak and how they'll react to you:

✔ What's the size of the audience?

✔ Is the audience required to attend?

✔ Are the people there to hear you or for some other reason?

✔ How much do they know about your topic?

✔ Will they be in a rush to leave?

✔ Will they be drinking?

✔ Will they be walking in and out as you speak?

✔ How have they responded to other speakers?

✔ What other speakers have they heard?

✔ What do they expect from you?

See the section 'Analysing Your Audience', later in this chapter, for a detailed discussion of how to suss out your listeners. (See Chapter 14 as well.)

Agreeing on a topic

You have a lot more control over your topic than you may suspect. Being asked to speak about a certain subject isn't the end of the discussion but just the beginning. If you don't like the topic, ask to change it. Many organisations will quickly accommodate your request. If you can't completely change the topic, try to slant it in a way that suits your needs.

Even when you're locked into a particular topic, you still have a lot of leeway in how to proceed. Suppose that you're a computer guru and you've been asked to speak about the latest upgrade to some software package that everyone wants to use. Will you give a broad overview? Will you give a list of specific tips for using it most effectively? Will you give a history of how it was developed? You can still essentially pick your topic because you can choose elements about the topic that was assigned to you.

Sometimes you may have free rein over the topic because the sponsoring organisation doesn't mind what you speak about. You may be given only the vaguest of guidelines – such as 'speak about business'. The organisation may just want you to show up and talk. (For more ideas on selecting a topic, see the section 'Analysing Your Audience' later in this chapter.)

Analysing Your Audience

How do you relate to an audience? You start by discovering as much about the people in the audience as possible – who they are, what they believe in, and why they are listening to you. This process is known as *audience analysis*.

The more information you can get, the more you can target your remarks to reflect your audience's interests. And by homing in on their concerns, you increase the likelihood that members of the audience will listen to you. Displaying your knowledge about an audience usually scores some points with them: They feel complimented that you bothered to learn about them.

Audience analysis also helps you develop your message. Such analysis structures the content of your presentation by shaping what types of arguments you should make; what the most effective examples will be; how complex your explanations can be; what authorities you should quote; and so on.

Discovering demographics

The first thing we always want to know about an audience is its size. Will it be 10 people, 100 people, or 1,000 people? The size of the audience determines many aspects of a presentation. For example, a large audience eliminates the use of certain types of visual aids and requires the use of a microphone. A smaller audience is often less formal. Certain gimmicks that work with a large group will seem silly with a small one. (Telling the audience to 'Turn around and shake hands with the person behind you' just doesn't work when the entire audience is seated in one row.)

The second thing we want to know is the general nature of the audience: What's the relationship of the audience members to each other? Do they all come from the same organisation? Do they share a common interest? We use this information to shape our presentations at a very basic level. If the audience have a lot in common, our presentations can use terms and concepts that they all understand. We won't have to explain as much as for an audience with more diverse backgrounds.

The next thing we want to find out is specific demographic data about audience members. Depending on the circumstances, you may want to check out some of the following details:

- Age
- Gender
- Education level
- Economic status
- Religious affiliations
- Occupations

✔ Ethnic mix

✔ Political inclinations

✔ Major cultural influences

Instead of wasting a lot of time impersonating a census taker, focus on the audience characteristics that will make a real difference to your presentation. Yes, you can collect plenty of information about the demographic mix of your audience, but you risk getting into 'analysis paralysis' – collecting so much information that you can't do anything useful with it. Yes, theoretically you may want to tailor your presentation to reflect every last characteristic of your audience but, in reality, you may not have the time or inclination to do that.

For example, suppose that you work for a drug company. You've been asked to present an overview of the company to a group of prospective investors. Is their age, sex, or religion going to affect what you say? Certainly you could think of ways to take advantage of your knowledge of these characteristics, but the shape of your talk will probably be a lot more heavily influenced by your knowledge of the audience's occupations and educational background. Are some of the prospective investors doctors? (They may know more about drugs than you do.) Are they professional investment advisors? Or are they wealthy individuals without a clue about corporate finance? (How sophisticated should you make your analysis of the 'numbers'?) You get the idea.

Discovering what the audience is thinking

While speakers tend to focus on audience census data, they tend to overlook audience beliefs, attitudes, and values. The reason is simple: Gleaning information about what the audience is thinking is difficult. Yet their beliefs, attitudes, and values will colour their interpretation of every aspect of your presentation.

What exactly do you need to know? In essence, you want to compose a mental profile of your audience – to know 'where they're coming from'. And the person who asked you to speak should help you find out. Here are some of the questions you want that person to answer:

- ✔ What is the audience's attitude to the subject of your talk?
- ✔ What is the audience's attitude toward you as the speaker?
- ✔ What stereotypes may the audience apply to you?
- ✔ May anyone have a hidden agenda?
- ✔ What values does the audience find important?
- ✔ Does the audience share a common value system?
- ✔ How strongly held are its beliefs and attitudes?

The answers to these questions may determine your approach to the subject.

Finding out what the audience knows

Want to start at the beginning with your audience? Then you'd better find out how much they already know. Two of the biggest mistakes speakers make are talking over the heads of their audiences and talking at a too-simple level. Ask the person who invited you to speak how sophisticated your presentation should be.

Here are some questions to ponder before you make your presentation:

- ✔ How sophisticated are the audience members about your topic?
- ✔ Will any experts be in the audience?
- ✔ Have the audience members heard other speakers talk about your topic?
- ✔ Why are they interested in your topic?
- ✔ Will they understand jargon related to your topic?
- ✔ Do they already know the basic concepts of your topic?

✔ Do they think they know a lot about your topic?

✔ How did they get the information that they already have about your topic?

✔ Are they familiar with your approach and attitude toward the topic?

The answers to these questions play a major role in how you construct your presentation. What your audience knows determines how much background you need to provide, the sophistication of the language you can use, and the examples you include.

Relating to Your Audience

Establishing rapport with your audience is your primary goal – a feeling of mutual warmth and a sense that you're on the same wavelength. The following sections present a few ways to achieve that goal.

Putting yourself in the shoes of your audience

Imagine that you're one of the members of the audience. What do they already know? What might they be interested in? Putting your audience at the heart of what you do – considering their needs and interests ahead of your own – is a great way to make them relate to you. In the following sections, we discuss some brilliant techniques for working out what your audience needs from you.

Focusing on what interests the audience

You don't have to ignore your own needs, but your needs won't be served if no one is listening. For instance, if your audience has been sitting and listening to hours of presentations all day, give them a break and cut your 60-minute speech down to 30 minutes – they'll thank you for it.

Discussing the world from the audience's point of view

Let the audience know that you can see the world or issue their way. Look for common experiences that both you and the audience share. For example, if your job has ever encompassed any of the duties of your audience, you could describe work situations that create a rapport and allow you to see the world from your audience's point of view. Or describe frustrating universal experiences such as traffic jams or dealing with faceless helplines.

 People like to hear data related to what they do. So if you don't have an experience to share, you can substitute a study. But first acknowledge that you don't have the experience – or you'll lose credibility. (Also see Chapter 3 for more on using research effectively.)

Making personal experiences universal

Although an audience wants to hear about a speaker's personal experience, using 'I' all the time can turn them off. You can end up sounding like a raging egomaniac. So go ahead and describe that experience – just find and emphasise the universal aspects of your personal experience. This advice applies to anyone using any kind of personal material – see the examples below:

- ✔ **Example 1:** 'You know, I used to be a plumber. Let me tell you about the time I flushed a fish down the toilet and it got blocked up.'

- ✔ **Example 2:** 'Did you ever have a job that you really hated but you couldn't quit because you needed the money? I used to be a plumber. And I couldn't quit because I needed the money. Let me tell you about what happened when a fish ended up getting flushed down a toilet and blocking it up.'

In the second example, the plumber tells the same story but the audience relates to him differently. Now he's not just a plumber talking about plumbing. He's a person who had a humorous experience with a lousy job – something everyone can understand.

Customising your remarks

Customising grabs the audience's attention and gets the audience involved in your speech. Tailoring your speech or presentation to a particular gathering makes the speaker a bit of an insider and lets the audience know that you went to the trouble of learning about them. And the good news is, a little (and we mean very little) customisation goes a long way. We've both given speeches where we made half a dozen references geared specifically to a particular audience and were showered with praise afterwards for the research we did to learn about the group. Make comments – humorous comments, praise, or just simple observations – about local businesses, the people you're speaking to, an organisation's history, or local news, events, or customs.

Use your imagination and consider what may impress you if an outsider referred to it.

Don't be offensive! If you're going to use a name of someone in or related to the group, clear it with a senior person at the organisation first. If you plan on poking fun at anything else local, discuss it with someone first to avoid inadvertently offending someone in the audience.

Pushing their buttons

Purposely work in a reference to a hot topic – a source of minor controversy with the audience. Find an issue that affects the entire audience, not one that only affects key players and that no one else would understand. In addition, make sure that the issue isn't too controversial to mention – your contact will probably be reliable here.

A favourite example is when one of us suggested that an audience ease up on memo and report writing. 'You're wasting too much photocopy paper,' Malcolm explained. The room burst into laughter and applause. Why? The people in the audience, employees of a big business, had been ordered to reduce their use of copier paper as a cost-saving measure. The comment wouldn't have been funny anywhere else. But here the audience thought it was ridiculous and appreciated the joke.

One of the simplest ways to find a hot topic is to ask your contact whether any recent or pending legislation or initiatives will negatively affect the audience. When the answer is yes, you have your issue.

Acknowledging what the audience is feeling

If you're speaking under any special circumstances, acknowledge those circumstances. Is the audience sweltering in a hot, stuffy room? Would the audience prefer to be anywhere but listening to you? Has the audience made certain assumptions about you? Get the issue out in the open or it will remain a barrier between you and your audience.

Identifying and addressing audience subgroups

Keep in mind that an audience may be made up of numerous subgroups – each with its own special needs and agendas. To create rapport with your entire audience, you need to include something for each of them.

A common example of this situation is the convention dinner attended by spouses. Half the audience is made up of people with the same occupation – engineers, doctors, whatever. The other half – the spouses – fall into two major categories: Those who have careers outside the home and those who perhaps look after the family full time. So you immediately have three subgroups. The spouses with careers can probably be even further subdivided.

Highlighting the benefits of what you've got to say

Make sure that the audience knows what they're going to get out of your speech. Identify and emphasise the benefits early in your talk and issue frequent reminders.

All audience members subconsciously ask themselves how a speech benefits them. They wonder if they will hear anything to help them save or make money; save time; or reduce stress, anxiety, ambiguity, and confusion. Sex and health are also topics of universal interest. These subjects span age, gender, culture, and geographic boundaries.

Chapter 3

Making the Most of Research

*T*he longest journey begins with a single step. So don't procrastinate. Don't put off until tomorrow what you really need to be starting today. If you have a presentation to make, get started on it. Open a book of quotations. Go to the library. Tap into the Internet. Call a museum. Do something. Do anything. Just get started.

Of course, you need to know *where* to get started – where to find the information to create your speech or presentation. Whether you're looking for a topical idea, major points to include or material such as jokes, quotes, statistics, and stories, you're going to need to do some research. In this chapter, we give you some starting points and techniques for basic research. (You can also find these techniques useful for finding the presentation material described in Chapter 5.)

Gathering Sources

An old philosopher once said that hearing a speaker who met an old philosopher is more interesting than hearing a speaker who read about one. He was right. People like to hear firsthand accounts of events and experiences when possible. And if you haven't spoken to the philosopher yourself, research usually turns up someone who did.

When you speak with the philosopher, you've got a primary source. When you read about someone who spoke with him, you've got a secondary source. Both types of sources are valuable. In this section we show you how to find sources that provide the information you need to create an effective presentation. Some are primary. Some are secondary. All of them are worth exploring.

Mining yourself for material

If you're old enough to give a presentation, you're old enough to have life experiences that you can use in it – personal anecdotes, war stories, insights, and observations. These are often the most interesting parts of your presentation and what the audience listens to closely and remembers. But how do you find these stories? Even though they're in your own head, many people have trouble getting them out. In the next two sections, we share with you some top tips on how to identify personal stories that can work in your presentation.

Creating new personal material

No matter what you discuss, you can always find an easy way to develop personal material. If you don't have any personal anecdotes that directly relate to your topic, simply go out and get some. Check out these examples:

  ✔ **If you plan on mentioning new house building projects as an economic trend indicator,** just drive around and count the number of housing developments you see under construction. Now you've got a personal experience that you can fit to your data. You can say, 'One of the most important indicators of our economic future is house building projects. As I drove to work the other day, I counted 15 houses under construction. Each one was swarming with workers sawing, hammering, and nailing; piles of wood and bags of cement covered each site; JCBs pulled in and out, hauling earth away; architects studied plans; a chap stopped by to sell lunch to the construction workers. It's amazing how much economic activity building a house can generate. So it's good news that house building programmes nationally have increased x per cent during the past year.'

✔ **If you plan on speaking about television,** just watch some. You can say, 'The other day I was turned off the moment my TV was turned on. It's not just the adverts, which were endless, or the repeats, which were, well, repetitive. The worst thing was the constant barrage of reality shows. If that's reality, I'm ready for fantasyland.'

✔ **If you plan on discussing politics,** just attend a local government meeting. You can say, 'A famous MP once said "All politics is local." I saw what he meant when I went to a local council meeting. It doesn't get more local than that. Every pothole, crack in the pavement, and overgrown tree seemed to come up in their discussions. And the politics behind these issues was fascinating; and just as complex as national political issues. Because when you get to the heart of it, politics is really about problem solving.'

Using what you already have

Of course, everyone knows that the easiest and most accessible material is the material you already possess. For example, if you're a teacher and you have an anecdote about the weird and whacky excuses your students make when they're late for school, you can use the story to illustrate your point about the need to take responsibility and not make excuses. This technique works especially well if your audience is filled with teachers or people that have to manage others and oversee team projects.

You can add even more power and punch to the anecdote and reach a wider audience if you unleash the anecdote's emotions. You can emphasise the *frustration* you felt when the students made their excuses. Then, even if your audience members aren't teachers, they'll understand what you mean because everyone can relate to frustration.

To find truly emotive material that an audience can connect with, try jotting down some basic emotions – love, anger, fear, hate, embarrassment, and so on – and then thinking of personal experiences that have caused each emotion. For example, think about experiences that made you angry. If you get stuck, narrow it down to specific situations. Try to remember situations about your work or family or school or football team that made you angry. After you find a good anecdote based on anger, write it down and edit it until it sounds pithy and interesting.

Interviewing people

One of the best, and most neglected, sources of primary material is other people. They have stories, experiences, and insights. You just have to interview them to get hold of this vast source of information. Writers and journalists do it. Police do it. Even game show hosts do it. Speakers and presenters, however, tend to ignore interviews as a source of information, which is a mistake.

Arranging and conducting an interview is no big deal. People love to talk about their work and hobbies. If you have to speak about cars, you can call a car dealer, tell them that you'll be giving a presentation about cars, and ask if they could spend five minutes talking with you. Most people won't refuse your request. They'll be delighted to give you information. Whatever your topic happens to be, interview a few people in that profession or industry.

Now let's talk about the interview. Often, people end their interviews by asking the following two questions: 'Is there anything you think I should have asked that I didn't?' and 'Do you want to add anything?' While these questions don't always yield much useful information, they could just possibly give you some additional details about your subject.

Another approach exists – questions that make a person dig deep and reveal fresh information that common questions can't produce. Try asking: 'What do you know now about (the topic) that you wish you knew when you were starting out?' This question becomes especially useful in situations when you may have less than a minute to conduct the interview – talking to someone in a lift, grabbing someone at a business function, meeting a celebrity on a plane, and so on. If you can ask only one question, ask this one.

Personal anecdote checklist

Personal anecdotes are among your most valuable assets as a speaker. They gain a lot of attention because they're real. So stockpile as many anecdotes as you can remember. Need some help recalling an anecdote based on a real-life experience? The following list will help jog your memory:

- Your most embarrassing experience
- The angriest you've ever been
- The most inappropriate letter you've ever received
- Your first date
- The strangest habit of a friend, relative, or co-worker
- The stupidest thing you've ever heard
- Your first day on the job
- The worst boss you've ever had
- The saddest thing that ever happened to a friend
- The biggest mistake you ever made

- A strange dream
- The most bizarre thing you've ever seen or heard
- Your wildest holiday story
- The weirdest thing that ever happened at a business meeting
- Eating out: Strange restaurants, incompetent waiters, awful food, poor service
- The trials and tribulations of relatives
- Learning to drive
- School: Teachers, lessons
- University or college: Your fellow students, lecturers, exams
- Anecdotes your parents told you
- Your first job interview
- Something that seems funny now but didn't when it happened
- The strangest gift you've ever received

Utilising the library

Everyone knows that the library is packed full of research and reference tools. But while everyone else hits the reference shelf, try this unusual advice: Make the *children's section* your first stop at the library. A children's book about your topic can be the best way to begin an outline because it will probably cover most of the key points of your topic clearly.

For example, let's say you have to give a presentation about minerals. A children's book may have chapters discussing: how minerals form, minerals from the ocean, minerals from the earth, precious minerals and gemstones, minerals used in construction, and so on. Each chapter could potentially be a major point in your talk. Or you could use the chapter titles to help you narrow down the scope of your topic.

Reading the Financial Times

If you're talking about business, read the *Financial Times*. This paper's a great source of statistics, anecdotes, and examples for just about any sector or field. The *Financial Times* contains plenty of news about what's going on elsewhere in the world as well.

Leading into your presentation with a topical example from the news can be a great idea because your audience may already have read or heard about it. A buzz may already exist about the topic, which may hopefully carry over into the buzz around your presentation, too.

Dialing up databases

Hopefully you're not still living in the Dark Ages of research by avoiding computers. Computers can dramatically speed up your research for a presentation. In almost any public or school library, you can find computers equipped with electronic databases that provide an enormous source of easy-to-locate information. You just type a word or phrase into the computer, and the computer searches through hundreds or thousands of journals. Then it spits out a list of relevant citations.

Okay, maybe you need five minutes to learn the computer commands, but doing so is still easier than searching through a thousand journals by hand. Besides, if you go to the library, you can usually find librarians who are happy to show you how. Or just go to the children's section and ask the nearest 11-year-old – she can probably work it better than you can anyway. If you want to know more about computerised researching of all kinds, get a copy of *Researching Online For Dummies,* 2nd Edition, by Reva Basch (Wiley).

How much does searching electronic databases cost? Not necessarily anything. A recent trip to a local university library
revealed that dozens of electronic databases are available.
Often, databases are free to search. The fee may come into
play when you want to print something out, and will differ
from library to library. Don't be shy about ringing ahead and
speaking to the library staff to figure out how much it costs
before you trek down there.

If you want to pay for information, you can subscribe to commercial electronic databases such as nexis.com (an extensive
collection of newspapers, periodicals, financial information,
and related materials) and lexis.com (same information, plus
law-related resources), both from LexisNexis, a division of the
big publisher Reed Elsevier, Inc.

Getting Someone Else to Do Your Research – For Free

Yes, you really can get other people to do some of your
research free of charge. No, you don't have to trick them, you
don't have to beg them, and you don't have to know any
secret handshakes or passwords. You can easily find people
who get paid by others to do research for you.

Checking out reference librarians

The most valuable resource at any library isn't found in a collection of books or periodicals but behind a desk answering
questions. This resource is the *reference librarian*. This person
doesn't know everything, but a good one knows how to find
anything.

Don't be shy. Tell the reference librarian what you're working
on and what you're looking for. They can provide invaluable
assistance in directing you to the appropriate resources and
can save you a tremendous amount of time when you're
beginning to prepare your speech or presentation.

Find out whether the reference librarian will answer your questions over the telephone. Many libraries provide this convenient service – take advantage of it. If you want to speak with someone at a library in another part of the country, all it costs is the price of a telephone call. Yes, this fact's obvious, but most people don't think of it.

All kinds of libraries employ reference librarians – everything from university libraries to corporate and association libraries.

Talking to museum research staff

Major museums have large research staffs devoted to pursuing knowledge about their specialised areas of interest. These staff members can be an incredible resource for presentation material. Phone them – they enjoy sharing their knowledge.

Researching on the Web

The Web is the Wild West of knowledge and information – an untamed frontier that keeps expanding faster than anyone can rein it in. And while the Web's full of gold mines and oil wells, you don't see a lot of signs pointing you in the right direction. So, in this section, we direct you to some useful Web sites so you can research topics, find visual aids, and even improve the delivery of your speech.

Accessing the best Web sites

If we had to give a talk on a desert island and we could only bring a handful of Web sites with us, these are our big choices.

✔ **Virtual Reference Library** (www.bl.uk/collections/ wider/vrlnew.html): This is a great general reference to materials available on the Web. A lot of stuff on the Web is written by North Americans, so you may be glad to hear that the focus of this reference Web site is primarily on sources that are of relevance to the United Kingdom. The materials have mainly been selected by staff at the British Library.

✔ **Office Humour.com** (www.office-humour.co.uk):
Plenty of American Web sites provide material about
funny laws in Wisconsin or strange things to do on a
'sidewalk'. But this Web site provides quotes, articles,
cartoons, and one-liners aimed at the British. So if you
want to use humour but worry about your ability to tell
jokes, you can find plenty of material on this Web site on
a variety of subjects.

✔ **Museum of Humor.com** (www.museumofhumor.com):
This is an amazing resource, albeit with a distinctly
American bias. The quotes and anecdotes may not be
of much use, but it does have indispensable writing tools
such as rhyme generators, simile generators, cliché
lists, phrase finders, Today in History, Guinness World
Records, and new word generators. A special section for
clergy has hundreds of sermons about humour, as well as
searchable databases of sermon-appropriate humour.

And if you have to use statistics in a talk, check out
'Calculated Humor' in the Exhibits section of the museum.
It provides tools for making statistics less boring and more
entertaining. (Just to see the Penguin-O-Matic Convertor
is worth the visit. It converts weights and distances into
numbers of penguins.) If you can navigate your way
around some of the Americanisms, this Web site is well
worth a visit to spruce up how you deliver your presentation material.

✔ **Wikipedia.com** (www.wikipedia.org): Wikipedia is a
free online encyclopedia that anyone can edit. Since its
inception in 2001, it has accrued literally millions of articles on just about any topic you may need to look up. In
addition to being free, this site's updated much more regularly than print encyclopedias, so you'll be able to find
articles on many leading-edge topics that could take
many months to get into print.

Getting the most out of Web researching

The Web can be a bit overwhelming, even if you know what
you're looking for. So, we've added some tips to make your
electronic research a little easier and more productive. To

avoid following Alice down an electronic rabbit hole, try the following:

- ✔ **Search engines:** An entire book could be devoted to search engines now available on the Web, but we'll just mention one – www.google.co.uk. Now the most popular search tool in cyberspace, Google is easy to use and comprehensive. Simply type a search term into the search box, and Google brings up enough links related to the topic that you could research from this search engine alone for days. Google even has an option for selecting only Web sites from the UK if you want to make the search more focused.

Usually, Google lists the most relevant links first. So, rather than clicking onto each link provided on every single page, glance through the summaries of each link on the first couple of pages. After you've found the ones most relevant to what you're looking for, then you can begin clicking away.

If you want to check out additional search engines, go to www.searchenginewatch.com/links. You can find enough to keep you busy for life.

For the best results, make your search terms as specific as possible to filter out thousands of useless links and to increase the chances that you find what you want. For example, a search for 'eulogy' produces better results than a search for 'public speaking' if you're looking for information about eulogies.

- ✔ **Web rings:** One of the best-kept secrets about conducting research on the Internet is the Web ring. A Web ring is a group of linked Web sites devoted to a similar topic. If you can find a Web ring related to your interests, you have an instant goldmine of relevant information. For example, say you're giving a talk about smoking and cancer. You could start by typing 'smoking' and 'cancer' into the search form at www.webring.org. It finds two Web rings that perfectly fit your criteria. And other Web rings exist that contain related (but not perfectly related) materials, too.

- ✔ **News Archives:** Many traditional sources of information – newspapers, magazines, newsletters, and so on – are represented on the Web. Even better, many of them have online archives that let you search through old editions. Use these sites to get started:

- NewsDirectory.com (`http://newsdirectory. com/archive/press/`): Here you'll find a long list of links to searchable newspaper archives.

- FindArticles.com (`www.findarticles.com/PI/ index.jhtml`): This index claims to have more than 3.5 million articles from 700 publications. You can search it by topic or keyword.

Finding visual aids

Need a picture for a slide, overhead, or PowerPoint presentation? The Web has almost anything you may want. You can find the best material at the following sites:

- **ImageFinder** (`http://sunsite.berkeley.edu/ ImageFinder`): A large collection of images (and the rules for using them) is available at the Berkeley Digital Image SunSite ImageFinder. It provides search forms for 11 databases of specialised images including photographs and images from the Library of Congress, Smithsonian Institution, and the National Library of Australia.

- **Clipart.com** (`www.clipart.com`): This site includes easy-to-search databases of well over a million clipart images and over 100,000 photos. The bad news is you have to pay for access. The good news is you don't have to pay much.

- **PowerPoint templates**: Thousands of professionally designed PowerPoint templates are available on the Web. And they're free! Find them by typing 'free PowerPoint templates' into any search engine. Get started by checking out the following sites (also check out Chapter 10 for more on PowerPoint presentations):

  - `www.soniacoleman.com/templates.htm`

  - `www.websiteestates.com/ppoint.html`

  - `www.presentersuniversity.com/ downloads.php`

Picking up performing tips

The Web not only has great sites for researching and writing a presentation, but it also has great sites that can show you how to *deliver* your presentation.

On the Web, you have access to thousands of hours of speeches and presentations; you can review which delivery techniques work and which don't; you can listen to other people's timing and pacing; and in many cases, you can hear how the audience responded.

You can use any search engine and find a large assortment of speeches. Or you can get ideas for gestures, movements, and other delivery techniques by watching and listening to speeches on the following sites:

- ✔ **History Channel Archive of Speeches** (`www.history channel.com/speeches/index.html`): This collection includes speeches by everyone from Mahatma Gandhi and Anwar Sadat to Richard Nixon and Queen Elizabeth II.

- ✔ **Podcast.net** (`www.podcast.net/`): Podcasts are short Web-enabled broadcasts that you can download. Try typing your search terms into the search box on Podcast and then you can watch someone else talk you through your topic.

Chapter 4

Organising Your Presentation

*T*he standard advice for organising a presentation or speech is: Tell the audience what you're going to say, then tell them, and then tell them what you've told them. We've heard many consultants offer this advice to their clients, look meaningfully into their eyes like they've just delivered some great insight, and then wait to be hailed as geniuses. But the problem with the tell-tell-tell formula is that it doesn't really tell you anything. (How's that for irony?) This advice is like telling someone that you build a ship by assembling a load of material so that it will float while you're in it. Okay, great. But how do you do that?

This chapter provides a detailed look at how to organise a presentation. We tell you everything from how to decide what to tell an audience, to how to arrange what you tell an audience, to how much to tell an audience. Actually, this is a tell-all chapter.

Selecting Material to Include

Before you can organise your presentation, you must first choose the material for it (see Chapters 3 and 5 for more on researching and finding material). But your real task is deciding what *not* to use. No matter what your topic, you'll always be able to find a lot more material than you'll have time to discuss. And, more importantly, audiences have a limit to how much material they can absorb. Here are a few guidelines to keep in mind when choosing what material to include:

✓ **Select a variety of material.** You know the expression 'variety is the spice of life'? Applied to speeches, it means using a mix of types of material – anecdotes, statistics, examples, quotes, and so on. A variety of material makes your speech more interesting. It also increases the chance that each member of your audience will find something appealing .

✓ **Keep your audience in mind.** Choose material that your audience will understand and find interesting. The question isn't what you know about the topic. It's what does the audience need to know in order to make your presentation a success.

✓ **Carry a spare – always.** Keep some material in reserve – an extra example, statistic, or anecdote. You never know when you'll need it, especially in a Q&A session following the talk.

Following Patterns of Organisation

Imagine that someone hands you a piece of paper that says 'm', 'd', 'u', 'y', 'm'. It doesn't seem to mean much. (Unless the letters are supposed to be an eye test.) Now assume that the person hands you the paper with the letters arranged as 'd', 'u', 'm', 'm', 'y'. Is your reaction a little different? Congratulations, you've recognised a pattern.

Patterns play a critical role in how we assign meaning and how we interpret messages. You could read a lot of perceptual psychology theory to figure out this stuff, but we'll let you off the hook and skip it. Suffice it to say that human beings have a natural tendency to organise information into patterns. The way we shape those patterns determines much of the outcome of our communications with each other. So, the patterns you put into your presentation play a vital role in how well your audience understands what you're communicating.

Sticking to two key rules

If you want the pattern to strengthen your presentation as much as possible, abide by the following two rules.

Make the pattern obvious

Have you ever seen those pictures that are all little dots? You know, the ones that you can't tell what the picture is supposed to be until you hold it close to your face? And then you're supposed to be able to see an image? Yes, the dots form a pattern because some people see the image, but the pattern really isn't obvious – at least to us and many other people who have never perceived the image.

Keep this fact in mind when you put together a presentation. You don't want a 'little dot' pattern that won't be recognised by everybody. You want a pattern that your whole audience can perceive. Your presentation isn't an intelligence test. You don't want to find out whether your audience is smart enough to discover your hidden structure. You want to make sure that your pattern is obvious so that your audience can perceive it – easily. Your pattern can never be too obvious.

Choose an appropriate pattern

Consider your topic and audience when choosing a pattern. What pattern will best help get your message across? For example, if you're talking about the history of a boundary dispute in your neighbourhood, a chronological pattern probably makes more sense than a theory/practice pattern. (See the section 'Checking out commonly used patterns', later in this chapter, for more information on types of patterns you can use.)

Checking out commonly used patterns

Although patterns are infinite in variety, certain ones appear over and over again. Here are a few of the most common patterns for presentations:

- ✓ **Problem/solution:** State a problem and offer a solution. For example, your presentation to a school's board of governors criticises the poor physical condition of the school. You then talk about a property scheme that could alleviate some of the financial pressures. What you emphasise depends on what the audience members already know. Do you need to make them aware of the problem or do they already know about it? Are there competing solutions? And so on.

- ✓ **Chronological:** If you plan to speak about a series of events (the history of accidents at that corner where you want a stop sign), organising your speech in a past/present/future pattern makes it easy to follow.

- ✓ **Physical location:** You may want to use this pattern if you're talking about things that occur at various locations. If you plan on giving the company orientation speech to new employees, you can divide the talk by floors (first floor, second floor, third floor), buildings (Building A, B, and C), or other physical areas (European operations, North American operations, Asian operations).

- ✓ **Extended metaphor or analogy:** This pattern uses a comparison of two items as a way of organising the entire presentation and is commonly used in speeches given by teachers or trainers. 'Today I'll talk about how giving a presentation is like the flight of an airplane. We'll talk about the takeoff, the landing, the flight, the passengers, and the control tower. The takeoff is the introduction . . .'

- ✓ **Cause/effect:** You state a cause and then identify its effect. This pattern is common in scientific presentations but it also works well for identifying where fault may lie. 'The southern region decided to listen to some management consultant this quarter. So it instituted new procedures, bought new expense-reporting software, and made a commitment to innovative sales methods. As a result, its gross sales declined by 50 per cent, and its margins shrank by 10 per cent.' (But the consultant had record profits.)

✔ **Divide a quote:** Each word of a quote becomes a section of the speech. Clergy often use this technique in sermons. 'The Bible says, "Wisdom is better than rubies". What does this really mean? Let's start with wisdom. Is it just your IQ? No. Most of us know people who have a high IQ who aren't very wise.' This technique is also frequently used by motivational speakers and sales trainers.

✔ **Divide a word:** Pick a word and build your speech around each letter of the word. 'Today, I'm going to talk about "LOVE". "L" stands for laughter. Laughter is very important in our lives because . . .' This pattern is popular with clergy, inspirational speakers, and consultants.

✔ **Theory/practice:** Start by explaining what you thought would happen – the theory. Then describe the actions taken and what actually happened – the practice. You can use this pattern when talking about something that didn't turn out as planned by explaining the big gap between theory and practice.

✔ **Topic pattern:** This is a free-form pattern that can be used for any type of speech. You divide your topic into logical segments based on your own instinct, judgement, and common sense. For example, you may use this pattern in a presentation on the topic of humour. The segments are: Why humour is a powerful communication tool, how to make a point with humour, and simple types of non-joke humour anyone can use. This easy-to-follow pattern makes sense for the material.

Packaging and bundling

One of the most powerful ways to organise information is in the form of a numerical list. For example, you can say, 'I have some good ideas'. Or you can say, 'I have four good ideas. The first is . . .' The number makes the statement much stronger. Because the audience tends to keep track of numbers, using them grabs their attention, keeps their attention, and helps them follow along and understand what you say.

You can use this technique to organise your entire presentation, such as 'Ten Ways to Increase Productivity'. Or you can use it for individual segments, such as, 'We've talked about the importance of humour, how to write a joke, and how to tell a joke. Now let's talk about six simple types of humour that don't require comic delivery.'

Don't go overboard – keep your lists short. If you make the list too long, you can actually lose the audience. Suppose your boss walked into a meeting and said, 'I've found 50 ways to raise revenue. The first is . . .' How would you feel after you realised he was going to discuss every one of them?

Creating Your Outline

An outline is a blueprint for your talk. It lets you see what points you're making, how they're related to each other, and whether they're arranged in a proper order. A good outline shows you how to construct a good speech. And like a blueprint for a building, an outline for a talk can take many shapes and forms.

Figuring out when to start your outline

You have two basic choices regarding when to make an outline: Make the outline before you've written your presentation or after you've written it. People disagree on which way is best. But here's the secret. The best way is the one that works for you. Consider the differences between writing the outline before or after you write the text of your presentation, and then decide which approach works best for you:

 ✔ **Before you write the presentation:** With this approach, you focus on your purpose and identify the ideas that will achieve that purpose. Then you turn the ideas into major and minor points and fit them into an outline structure. Only then, when you can see exactly what you'll say, do you begin to flesh it out. This is an absolutely logical way to proceed. If the outline makes sense, it helps ensure that the content of your presentation will make sense.

✔ **After you write the presentation:** Alternatively, you may just plunge right into developing your material word for word. You could think about the order in which you'd tell it to a friend, as well as what examples you'd use. Then write the outline after the presentation is written. This approach enables you to discover any flaws in your presentation's structure so that you can rewrite where appropriate.

Deciding the number of points to include

The number of points in an outline should reflect the number of points in your presentation. So you need to decide how many points to divide your material into. To make the best decision, follow these guidelines:

✔ **Decide what the audience needs to know.** Determine which points are absolutely essential for you to include in your message. And we mean *absolutely* essential, as in, if one of these points were omitted, your speech couldn't succeed.

✔ **Avoid putting in too much information.** Many people try to pack too much information into a single speech. But a limit exists as to how much an audience member can absorb. Figuring out how much is too much may sound tricky but the following two guidelines can make the process easier on you:

• **Use no more than seven main points.** People disagree over the maximum number of points that you should have in a talk, but the highest number that we've found works in practice is aroundseven. Less is usually better. The amount of time you have to speak is also a critical factor. Many experts suggest three major points for a half-hour talk.

• **Reorganise to reduce the number of points.** You've gone through your material and found 15 main points that are absolutely essential. Don't even think about doing your speech that way. First, make sure that you really can't lose a few of them. Second, reorganise the points so that they're included under fewer headings. Think of 5 to 7 major points under which your 15 points can be subcategorised.

Timing

Most people associate *timing* with how to tell a joke. But by timing, we mean how much time it takes to deliver the talk you've written. Does it fit the time slot you've been given? Check out the following sections to find out the important concepts of timing.

Setting the length of your speech

William Gladstone once observed that a speech need not be eternal to be immortal. His point is well taken: Longer doesn't mean better or more meaningful in the world of presenting and speaking in public. Waffle on for too long and you'll simply bore your audience. Follow these guidelines to make sure you set an appropriate length of time for your presentation:

- ✔ **Don't feel obligated to fill your entire time slot.** Use your common sense. You shouldn't stretch your speech to fill an hour-long time slot if you can get the job done in just 45 or 50 minutes. Your speech can end up sounding disorganised, and your points can get hard to follow when you throw in extra information just to cover another 15 minutes. On the other hand, one of us recently spoke at a conference where another speaker, who was slotted for a one-hour speech, completed his talk in ten minutes. As you can imagine, the conference organisers were less than thrilled.

  Although concluding early can thrill your audience, concluding late can have the opposite effect. Even running on by just an extra five minutes could make the audience impatient and possibly angry. Your audience members are busy, and they don't appreciate a speaker putting them behind schedule. They expect you to be done on time, so don't disappoint them.

- ✔ **Twenty minutes is a good length.** If you can choose how long you'll speak, pick 20 minutes. This gives you long enough to cover a lot of information thoroughly, let the audience get to know you, and make a good impression. And the time's short enough to do all that before the audience's attention span reaches its outer limit.

Polishing your timing

Einstein's theory of relativity may say that time and distance
are identical, but many public speakers apparently disagree.
They just can't go the distance in the time they've been allotted. You certainly don't want to join that group. So check out
the following tips to ensure that you and your audience finish
at the same time:

- **Estimate the time from the length of your script:** As a
  rule of thumb, one double-spaced page of 10-point type
  equals two minutes of speaking time. So preparing a standard 20-minute talk is like writing a 10-page essay. (Keep
  that in mind when the person inviting you to speak says
  it will be easy to do.)

- **Convert practice time into a realistic estimate:** Many
  speakers practise their speech aloud to get an idea of
  how long it will take to deliver. But be careful: For every
  minute that you practise your speech alone, it'll take you
  about a third longer when you speak in front of people.
  We tend to slow down because we wait for feedback and
  have to focus on making eye contact with the audience
  as well as presenting our materials. So a 30-minute talk
  could take 40 minutes. The duration of your presentation
  may increase by as much as 50 per cent when you speak
  to an audience of several hundred people. And if you're
  frightened when you face an audience, you may speak
  faster than you did while practising. (See Chapters 11
  and 20 for help eliminating stage fright.)

- **Make an adjustment for humour:** If you use humour in
  your talk and it's effective, part of your speaking time
  may be consumed by audience laughter and applause.
  Don't forget to account for that time, especially for large
  audiences numbering in the hundreds of people. With a
  large group, some of the group may get the joke straight
  away. Others may get it a little later. And the third group
  laugh simply because everyone else is laughing. So if
  your material is genuinely funny, be prepared to allow
  extra time for the waves of laughter or applause.

- **Be prepared to cut:** You were told that you'd have 30
  minutes to speak. But the meeting doesn't go as planned
  and the organiser says you have only 15 minutes. What
  do you do? Of course the biggest mistake would be to try

to cram your half-hour's worth of material into 15 minutes. Talking loudly and faster doesn't work! You will leave your audience with the impression that you are a bit manic. Perhaps worse, nothing will sink in.

✔ **Don't cut the conclusion:** When you need to cut part of your presentation, don't cut the conclusion. Your speech is like the flight of a plane, and the passengers are your audience. When you forgo the conclusion, you're attempting a crash landing. If you've been told in advance that your time will be shortened, cut material from the body of your talk. Eliminate some examples or even a main point if necessary. What if you need to cut while you're speaking and you're rapidly running out of time? Find a logical place to stop and sum up what you've already said. Even better, have a conclusion that you can go into from any point in your talk.

Organising Your Presentation Effectively

As many ways to organise presentations and speeches exist as there are people giving them. But one of the simplest and most effective is to use cards, as follows:

1. **Write ideas on cards.** Begin by writing down each idea you have on a separate card. Write on only one side of the card to leave lots of room for editing. Say you're writing a presentation about training courses at work. One card may say, 'Get graph from human resources on uptake of current courses'. You may scribble 'comments from trainers' and 'list of currently available courses' on other cards. By the time you're done, you may have dozens of cards.

2. **Pile the cards into patterns.** So now you have a couple of dozen cards full of ideas. What next? Spread them on a big table or the floor and look for patterns. Try to group them into piles. For example, one pile may be 'benefits of the current training programme', while another may be 'downsides of the current training programme'.

Short takes on long speeches

The long-winded speaker has inspired plenty of one-liners regarding the subject of public speaking. Here's a small sample:

✔ Many a public speaker who rises to the occasion stands too long.

✔ No speech is all bad if it's short.

✔ The longest word in the English language is 'And now a word from our guest of honour'.

✔ If the speaker won't boil it down, the audience must sweat it out.

✔ An after-dinner speech is like a headache – always too long, never too short.

✔ Having a train of thought is alright if you also have a terminal.

✔ Second wind: What a speaker acquires when he says, 'In conclusion.'

✔ A speech is like a love affair – any fool can start one, but it takes a lot of skill to end one.

3. **Sequence the cards in each pile.** Say you end up having six or seven cards in each pile. Keep rearranging the cards within a particular pile until you have a good flow between the cards. In doing so, you may find a gap in the sequence – say that cards 1, 2, and 3 work well but card 4 doesn't fit and needs rewriting before it flows into card 5. Another tip is to number the cards. Doing so helps you keep track of them much more easily. Perhaps label the piles A, B, C, and so on, and then number the cards 1, 2, 3 within each pile so they'll be A1, A2, A3, B1, B2, B3. This system doesn't mean A goes first, just that all the cards in that pile go together.

4. **Sequence the piles of cards.** Look at what you've got and see which pile is logical for starting your talk. Then look for the second, third, and so fourth, until all the cards are in the best order.

Part II
Preparing Your Presentation or Speech

'Next time you address our society, we'd be
very grateful if you <u>wouldn't</u> finish your speech
on a high note!'

In this part . . .

Great presentations and speeches don't happen by accident. Careful preparation is the key. In this part, we show you how to prepare a great presentation. We cover developing an outline, selecting and organising material, writing an attention-grabbing introduction, and creating a memorable conclusion. You also discover how to use statistics and quotations for maximum impact, as well as how to develop stories, examples, and analogies.

Chapter 5

Building the Content of Your Presentation

*A*fter you have a topic and an outline (see Chapter 4), you only have the skeleton of your presentation figured out. You still have to create the body of your talk by adding support to the outline you've created. Although searching for various forms of support for every point you plan to make sounds like a lot of sweat, you can consider this chapter the equivalent of a protein shake for presentation writing. We show you the proper techniques to ensure that you create the content to back up your points and build the presentation of your dreams.

Making Appeals to Your Audience

While speaking to your audience, making appeals can connect them to your topic as well as sway them to your line of thinking. Thus, this technique can be very important to your presentation. You can use logical appeals, emotional appeals, or both to bolster the effectiveness of what you say.

Using logical appeals

You base a logical appeal on rational evidence and arguments, appealing to the 'heads' of your audience. Think of Mr Spock from *Star Trek* or Sherlock Holmes – the ultimate practitioners of the logical appeal.

For example, say you're giving a talk about the need for a neighbourhood watch scheme. You could point out that a large number of burglaries has occurred over the last two years, that the unsightly vandalism causes an eyesore that decreases property prices, and that everyone's insurance premiums would actually go down if the neighbourhood watch scheme came into place. These are all logical reasons that will appeal to the common sense of the audience.

A logical appeal works best when you're trying to influence an audience of 'left brain' thinkers – engineers, scientists, and anyone else who won't be easily swayed by emotion.

Making emotional appeals

You base an emotional appeal on feelings and passions. Unlike the logical appeal, which appeals to the 'heads' of your audience (see the earlier section, 'Using logical appeals'), an emotional appeal speaks to their 'hearts'. Politicians often appeal to hearts when they use moving video footage or rousing music to accompany their presentations. An emotional appeal is supposed to tug at your heartstrings.

Say you're giving a talk about the need for a neighbourhood watch scheme. You could point out the terrible story of the old lady at the end of the street whose house was broken into and how precious mementoes of her late husband were stolen from her. You're not presenting a rational argument but describing her loss and hardship can appeal to the emotions of your audience.

An emotional appeal works best when your audience consists of people who like to take feelings, not just facts, into consideration when forming their opinions.

Finding Solid Forms of Support

This section isn't about tights and hosiery. Support refers to the items you use to prove and illustrate your points – the basic material that makes up your speech – stories, quotes, and statistics.

Because your support is the basic material for your speech, what kind you use, as well as how you use it, is very important. Three basic rules regarding forms of support are:

- ✔ **Make sure that your support really supports something.** Don't throw in quotes, statistics, and stories just to show off or beef up the length of your talk. Use them only to prove, clarify, or illustrate a point.

- ✔ **Use a variety of support.** Different people respond to different types of information. Some people like statistics; others like quotes and stories.

- ✔ **Remember that less is more.** Using one dramatic statistic gets more attention than three boring statistics. One great example makes more of an impact than two so-so examples.

Mastering the art of storytelling

Throughout history, people have passed down customs, ideas, and information by telling stories. We seem to be hard-wired to recognise and respond to this type of communication, which is why stories are so powerful when used in a talk.

Anyone can use a story, but using a *good* story and using it effectively sets you apart from the average speaker. Here are a handful of guidelines we've gathered together to give you some ways to use stories effectively in your presentations:

- ✔ **Tell stories for a purpose:** You should have a reason for telling a story. And the reason – a lesson, moral, or objective – should be obvious to the audience. Telling pointless stories is one of the quickest ways to turn off an audience. (Just think of how you feel when Auntie Jane corners you at Christmas after knocking back a few too many sherries.)

✔ **Tell personal stories:** You know how much you like to hear stories about yourself or people you know. So just think of all the attention your presentation could receive if you use stories about yourself or people familiar to your audience. Personal stories interest an audience much more than just plain facts.

If you don't have many personal stories or stories about real individuals to tell, you can still add personal stories to your talk. You can either use hypothetical stories or interview other people and tell their stories. Other people's stories are so simple to find and are such a great source of material that you shouldn't overlook them, although many speakers do. Audience members will also tell you stories after your speech. Collect the more relevant and interesting of these – don't forget to ask permission to use them, of course.

✔ **Tell success stories:** Nothing succeeds like success, and that includes success stories. Think of the stories that you liked as a child. Most of them ended with the words 'happily ever after'. Those words are the sign of a success story. People like to hear stories about how an idea or action worked out successfully.

✔ **Try out stories first:** The first time you tell a particular story shouldn't be when you're standing at a podium addressing your audience. You need to know how the story works – what kind of response it gets from others. So try stories out first on your friends, neighbours, colleagues, and anyone willing to listen. Their responses – body language, facial expressions, laughter, and other verbal and nonverbal responses – give you an idea of how to tweak the content, delivery, or timing of your story. The story should get better every time you tell it, and by the time you use the story in a speech, you should have a polished gem.

✔ **Develop more powerful stories:** You can make your stories more effective if you understand exactly how and why they affect an audience. To accomplish this task, ask yourself (and answer) the following questions:

- What's the objective, moral, lesson, punch line, or purpose of the story?

- What's the plain-English synopsis of what you're trying to get across?

- What are the beginning, the middle, and the end?

- Does the story have a people focus? Who are the main characters in the story? Why are they interesting?

- What is the sequence of events that makes the story work? Are there some facts or data that should be put into the story? Does the story as you currently tell it have too many facts and too much data? Do they really help the story or hurt it?

- What are the human factors in the story that make it interesting?

Making an impact with quotations

Quotes get immediate attention – especially when they're attached to a famous name. In today's sound-bite society, quotes provide a great way to make a strong impression in the minds of audience members, if you know how to use them effectively. Improve the quality of your presentation by following these guidelines the next time you include a quote in your speech:

✔ **Relate the quote to a point:** A quote should be used to make a point otherwise it's irrelevant – no matter how funny or insightful it is. Sometimes you may find a great quote that just doesn't fit, and you can't make it fit without reworking a great deal of your talk. Just accept the fact that the quote doesn't fit, and save it for your next talk.

Using quotes that have nothing to do with your topic can make you sound like a namedropper. The audience can tell when you're trying to appear smart by dropping names in your speech. Throwing around phrases, such as 'As Albert Einstein once said. . .' or 'According to Socrates. . .' sounds forced. While you're trying to sound smart, using such quotes often has the opposite effect.

✔ **Use a variety of sources:** Unless you're doing a tribute to a particular celebrity, no one wants to hear endless quotes from a single source. That type of repetition gets boring fast. If you're only going to quote the Dalai Lama, then why didn't you just get the Dalai Lama to give your speech? Mix it up a bit. Go ahead and quote the Dalai Lama, but quote Aristotle, Confucius, and Doctor Who, too.

✔ **Keep it brief:** You don't want to lose the conversational quality of your presentation, and a long quote starts to sound like you're reading it, even if you're not. Shorten lengthy quotes and tell the audience that you're paraphrasing. Just say, 'To paraphrase Mr Whoever', then say the shortened quote.

✔ **Use a simple attribution:** Just say, 'Mr So-And-So once said . . .' and give the quote, or give the quote and then say who said it. You can sound a bit ridiculous if you say 'quote . . . unquote' unless you're doing a dramatic reading from a court transcript.

✔ **Cite a surprising source:** You can bolster support for your argument in a powerful way by using quotes from an unlikely source. It's so unexpected for a Labour politician to support his position by quoting a Conservative, or a trade union leader to advance her cause by quoting management, or a Sunday morning vicar to prove his point by quoting the song lyrics of a boy band. Such startling contrasts always get attention and can be very effective.

✔ **Hedge your bets whenever you're in doubt:** If you're not sure who said the line that you're quoting, you don't have to delete the quote from your speech – you just have to know how to cover yourself. Simply say, 'I believe it was Mr Famous Name who once said. . .' or use the great cover phrase, 'As an old philosopher once said. . .' After all, everyone is a philosopher of one sort or another. So if you find out that the line came from Donald Duck, you can still argue that he was being philosophical.

Doing it by numbers

Benjamin Disraeli, one of our more notable Prime Ministers, famously once said, 'There are three kinds of lies: lies, damned lies, and statistics.' He may have overstated the case, but not by much. Statistics enable you to slice up reality in a way that suits your perspective.

Statistics and numerical data can provide some of the most influential support in your entire speech, but they commonly lose their impact because speakers use them ineffectively. Get your numbers to register on your audience's bottom line by checking out these suggestions:

- **Give your audience time to digest:** Most people can't process numbers as rapidly as they can process other types of information, so don't drown your audience in numerical data. Give your listeners time to digest each statistic; don't just spew numbers at them. If you don't space statistics out, the audience will – space out, that is. (An exception to this rule involves *startling* statistics; see the later bullet point in this list for a discussion of this exception.)

- **Round off numbers:** If you're telling aerospace engineers how to build a more efficient jet engine, then by all means, use exact numbers. But if exact numbers aren't critical to your subject matter or to your audience, give everyone a break – round them off. Your listeners don't need to know that the candidate you backed won with 59.8 per cent of the vote. Just say 60 per cent.

- **Use a credible source:** A statistic is only as impressive as its source. Did you get your numbers from the *Financial Times* or the *News of the World*? A big difference lies between the two.

What many people don't realise is that the *Financial Times* may not always be the more credible source. Credibility depends on your audience. You may be speaking to people who read the *News of the World* religiously and distrust the *Financial Times*, categorising it as a tool of the rich. Only your audience can bestow credibility upon a source. Keep that point in mind when you select your statistics.

- **Repeat key numbers:** If you want people to hear and remember an important statistic, say it more than once. Just think of the audience as a person you've wanted to date and who has just asked for your number. You wouldn't just say it once, would you?

- **Use startling statistics:** The big exception to the general rule that statistics are boring is the *startling* statistic. This term refers to numerical data that's so surprising that it just grabs your attention. A startling statistic is inherently interesting.

For example, if you were giving a speech about the need for more recycling, you might start by using this statistic from the `recycle-more.co.uk` campaign: In 2000, people in the UK bought 5 billion aluminium drinks cans. Apparently only 42 per cent of them were recycled. So 2,900,000,000 cans were thrown away, which is approximately 7,495,000 cans a day or over 331,000 cans every hour of every single day!

✔ **Relate the numbers to your audience:** Numbers are abstract concepts, and if you want to make an impact, you have to make the audience relate to the numbers you plan to discuss. To make numerical data more concrete, try the following techniques:

- **Put statistics into familiar terms:** Discuss numbers in a way that people can understand. Explain numbers in terms that have real meaning for your audience.

  For example, in the recycling example, the average household uses 3.2kg of aluminium cans a year – about 208 cans. Ask your audience to imagine 208 cans piled up on their kitchen table. Or, even better, bring in a pile of 208 cans to present them with a very real scene of what those statistics mean in practice.

- **Create a picture:** Transform your numbers into a concrete image so your audience can see the statistic. Paint a picture for them.

  Regarding the recycling of aluminium cans, the `recycle-more.co.uk` Web site tells us that if all the aluminium cans recycled in the UK last year were laid end to end, they would stretch from John O'Groats to Land's End 140 times. That fact should give your audience pause for thought.

- **Use analogies:** Turn your abstract statistics into easy-to-visualise images.

  In Britain, as in most of the Western world, the aging population is a crucial issue. Young people aren't having as many babies as they did a few decades ago. Which means that in the future fewer

workers will exist to pay for the pensions of the elderly. Right now it requires around four workers to
pay the pension of each elderly person. But in a
few years' time, as the whole population becomes
increasingly older, there'll only be two workers
available to pay for that pension. And all the while
the cost of that pension keeps swelling up like a
balloon. By the time the people currently leaving
school are ready for retirement, that pension cost
balloon may just well have burst.

- **Create visual aids:** If you have a great deal of
numerical data in your presentation, consider putting it into a visual format – using computer technology, slides, or overheads of charts or graphs. If
your audience members can see the data, they'll
find it much easier to digest. (See Chapter 10 for an
extended discussion of this topic.)

Clearing the air with definitions

If someone offered you a new job and said that they would pay
you a 'huge' salary, you'd be pretty excited, wouldn't you? But
the canny part of you might want to ask 'how huge exactly?'
Because what an employer defines as 'huge' might not be what
you define as huge. And, in the same way, audiences don't
always define words in the same way that you might.

If you don't want to risk confusing or annoying your audience,
make sure that you're all speaking the same language. The following list shows you a few ways to use definitions in a
speech to prevent misunderstandings:

✔ **Use the dictionary definition:** The simplest way to
define a term is to look it up in a dictionary and use the
definition in your presentation. For example, if you're
going to talk about ethics, then you might lead off by
saying,

'The *Oxford English Dictionary* defines ethics as the
science of morals in human conduct.'

✔ **Use your personal definition:** If you don't like the dictionary definition, then give the meaning of the term as
you define it.

For example, the *Oxford English Dictionary* defines quality as 'the degree of excellence of a thing'. However, you might say,

> 'How do I define *quality* in a news report or analysis? My measure is summed up in three words: *Accuracy*, *objectivity*, and *responsibility*.'

When a word is emotionally charged, some members of your audience may misinterpret your remarks unless you clearly explain *your* use of the term. For example, you may be talking about money. You could say that 'money is evil' and go on to say that the pursuit of money for its own sake can lead people down a path toward greed and selfishness. Or you could say that 'money is good' because it allows those people who have it to support those who do not. So always explain why you are taking a particular stance on an issue.

Unlocking concepts with analogies

An analogy is a comparison that highlights similarities (and differences) between two objects or concepts. An analogy provides one of the fundamental ways that we gain new knowledge. An analogy allows us to explain the unknown in terms of the known. When a toddler asks, 'What's heaven?' and you answer, 'It's like school, but there's only playtime and no homework', you're using an analogy.

Analogies are particularly well suited to presentations that teach, train, or educate an audience – any talk in which you're explaining something. They also provide an opportunity to add a touch of humour. For example, you're giving a talk about lack of leadership and might say, 'Leadership is like the Loch Ness Monster. You hear about it a lot, but no one sees it very often.' And then pause to wait for the laughs!

Getting heard with examples

Two of the most frequently used words in the world are 'for example'. We use these words to illustrate what we're talking about, which is why examples are probably the most common devices for supporting ideas and assertions.

You can use two types of examples in your speech: real and hypothetical. You base a real example on fact. You base a hypothetical example on imagination – the data's made up.

Real examples tend to be more powerful than hypothetical examples because they're, well, real. The example's something that actually exists that you can point to. Hypothetical examples are always subject to the criticism that they're not real. However, they can be very effective in presentations that involve philosophy, law, or theoretical concepts.

Regardless of whether you use real or hypothetical examples, if you want to get maximum mileage from them, don't ignore positive examples. Too often, speakers tell you what you shouldn't do, but they never say what you should do. So don't fall into this trap yourself. You can take a specific example and talk about how it went wrong and how it may have been handled differently. But if you're going to give just one side of the example, talk about the right behaviour and allude to the wrong one – and not the other way around. Don't leave the audience hanging.

Chapter 6

Getting Off on the Right Foot

· ·

In This Chapter

▶ Setting audience expectations

▶ Figuring out what to include in your introduction

▶ Discovering several different ways to get off to a great start

· ·

*O*ur model of making a presentation is like the flight of an airplane (which you'll hear about ad nauseam throughout this book). In this model, the introduction is equivalent to the plane's takeoff. You're the pilot. Your audience (the passengers) want your introduction to lead smoothly into the body of your talk (the flight). How you perform the introduction affects your credibility and determines the audience's mind-set for the rest of your presentation.

Making the best introduction depends on several factors. In this chapter, we discuss important concepts to consider before you write your next introduction. So check out the sections below to ensure your next introduction sets your audience up for a great flight.

Discovering What the Introduction Must Do

Since ancient times, presentations and speech writing experts have taught that an introduction has three basic functions. It must gain the attention of the audience. It must create rapport between the speaker and the audience. And it must provide reasons for the audience to listen to the speaker.

But the real purpose of the introduction is to *set the expectations of the audience*. Basic psychology tells us that the way we perceive things is very much affected by what we've been led to expect. So the introduction is critical – it determines how the audience interprets and reacts to everything else you say. And the introduction's also your best opportunity to shape the audience's reaction in your favour.

Yes, the introduction has to gain attention, lead into the rest of your talk, and perform all those other traditional functions you always hear about. But all of those functions are encompassed in setting expectations.

Your goal is to set the audience's expectations in your introduction and then *surpass* them. Doing so guarantees your presentation or speech will be a success.

Creating the Perfect Introduction

A journey of a thousand miles begins with a single step. That statement also applies to presentations – a talk of any length begins with the introduction. The following sections cover the steps that you must take in making this first leg of your journey.

Answering audience questions

The audience has several questions that they want answered within the first few minutes of your talk. Think of the questions journalists ask to report a story: Who, what, when, where, why, and how. Your audience wants to know those same things. So be sure to answer the following questions in your introduction:

- ✔ Who are you? (Do you have any experience or credentials?)
- ✔ What are you going to talk about?
- ✔ When will you be through?
- ✔ Where is this talk going? (Is there some sort of agenda, organisation, or structure?)

> ✔ Why should I listen? (Really a 'what' question – what's in it for me?)
>
> ✔ How are you going to make this interesting?

Including necessary background

If the audience needs certain information in order to understand what you'll be talking about, give it to them in the introduction. If your talk won't make sense unless audience members know the definition of a certain term or they're aware of a certain fact, tell them. Also, you may need to provide background about why you *won't* be covering a particular subject or subtopic – especially if the audience expects you to address it.

Using greetings and acknowledgements

Many speakers open talks with endless greetings and acknowledgements to the sponsoring organisation and key members of the audience. Boring! No one wants to hear you list the names of every dignitary on the dais. All right, sometimes you have to name names, but you don't have to do it as your opening line. If you must acknowledge a load of people, do it as the second item in your introduction – not the first.

Making your introduction the right length

The introduction should be no more than 10 to 15 per cent of your presentation. And it shouldn't be more than 4 or 5 minutes at the very most. Remember you're there to talk about your topic and not about you (unless you have been invited to talk about yourself, of course.) So avoid making the audience yawn – don't take forever.

Writing out your introduction

Write out your entire introduction word for word. Don't worry that you're just supposed to use key words or sentence fragments when writing the body of your presentation, or that a fully scripted presentation may sound strained. The introduction is an exception, and writing it out actually provides the following benefits to your presentation:

- ✔ **You can edit it into its best form.** If you just make a note that you're going to tell a certain story in the introduction, you don't write out or practise the story. You figure you already know it. Then when you tell it, you end up rambling; you don't economise words; and the story doesn't achieve its maximum impact.

- ✔ **You can deliver a successful intro even if you're anxious.** The introduction is the most anxiety-producing section of your presentation in terms of delivery. Stage fright is at its peak. If you get really nervous and your introduction is just a few key words, you may not even remember what they represent. Writing out the introduction word for word helps ensure that you'll carry it off successfully even if you suffer from a case of the jitters.

The introduction is the first part of your talk, but ideally you should write it last. Why? Because this section's an introduction. You need to know what you're introducing. After you write the body of your presentation and your conclusion, then you've got something to introduce.

Using the show biz formula

In planning your introduction, recalling the show biz formula never hurts: Strong opening, strong close, weak stuff in the middle. Your introduction is the strong opening. Your conclusion is the strong close. Those are the two parts of your presentation that have the most impact on how the audience remembers your performance. So make sure your introduction *is* strong.

Avoiding common mistakes

Sometimes what you don't say in your introduction is even more important than what you do say. Avoid starting on the wrong foot – especially if that foot is inserted in your mouth. Here are some common mistakes to avoid:

✔ **Saying 'Before I begin . . .'** This is a patently absurd phrase. It's like airline personnel who ask if anyone needs to preboard the plane. You *can't* preboard. After you start going on the plane, you *are* boarding. And as soon as you say, 'Before I begin', you've begun. If you want to make some comments before you get into the body of your presentation, try 'Before I get into the meat of my presentation . . .' or 'Before we get stuck into the topic, I'd like to say . . .'.

✔ **Getting the names wrong.** If you're acknowledging people, organisations, or places, such as towns or cities, make sure that you know their names and pronounce them correctly. No one likes to be called by the wrong name. Messing up names makes you look very unprepared, lowers your credibility, and makes the audience wonder what else you're going to screw up.

✔ **Admitting that you'd rather be anywhere else.** If we're in your audience, our immediate response is: 'So get out of here.' Yes, you may be in a position where you're giving a presentation that you don't want to give, but don't whine to the audience. No one wants to hear you moaning, and doing so doesn't help. You still have to give the presentation, and you just seem like a big baby.

✔ **Admitting that you're not prepared.** Doing so is insulting to your audience. If you're not prepared, why are you speaking? No one wants to waste time listening to someone who isn't prepared. Although this is common sense, a lot of speakers make this mistake. Why? They're really making excuses in advance. They know they're not prepared. They know their presentation will go down horribly, and they want the audience to know that they're really not a terrible speaker – they're just not prepared. The logic seems to be that if you alert the audience in advance that you know your presentation is going to be rubbish, somehow that improves your image. Wrong. You just seem like an idiot for being unprepared. If you're not prepared and you're going to speak anyway, just do it.

✔ **Admitting that you've given the identical presentation a million times for other audiences.** Even if your audience knows this fact, don't rub their faces in it. Every group likes to feel unique. Let your audience operate under the illusion that you prepared the talk especially for them. And if you're smart, you'll throw in just a couple of customised references to promote this illusion.

✔ **Using offensive humour.** A lot of speakers still labour under the myth that you've got to open with a joke. You don't. But if you do use this technique, don't tell a racist, ethnic, sexist, or off-colour joke. No faster way exists to turn off an audience.

✔ **Announcing that you had a ghostwriter.** Admitting this fact is like a magician showing how the tricks are done. Your audience likes to think they are hearing from you. Let them think so. Remember, a 'ghostwriter' is supposed to be invisible – you know, like a ghost.

✔ **Apologising.** Unless you accidentally activate the emergency sprinkler system, shut off the power for the room, or knock the podium off the stage, *never begin by apologising*. Apologising sets a horrible tone for audience expectations – they expect something bad. Why else would you be apologising? Plus, an apology draws attention to something the audience may not otherwise notice. If you don't start by apologising for your presentation, the audience may actually think what your saying is good. And if they don't think your presentation's good? You can always apologise later.

Breaking the ice

Presenters can introduce themselves in all sorts of weird and whacky ways. We've heard of a speaker who brings in an ice cube, puts it on a table, takes his shoe off, and smashes it onto the ice. Of course, he then goes on to say: 'Now that we've broken the ice, we can talk about...'

A music therapist of our acquaintance often starts by asking her audience to hum with her. Apparently, humming opens up the airways and gets people breathing more deeply, injecting a blast of oxygen into their systems and waking them up.

We even know of a professor who sings his introductions.

All of these techniques work very well for their audiences. But think very carefully before deciding to use an unusual introduction to your presentation. What you think is funny and attention-grabbing may just seem odd and inappropriate to the wrong audience.

Getting Started in Fifteen Fabulous Ways

No matter how the introduction begins, the effect that every speaker desires is the same – to knock the socks off the audience. You want your audience to focus their full attention on you and have them hanging on your every word. The big question is, how do you accomplish this feat?Well, no magic formula exists but there *are* lots of ways to begin. On the next several pages is a list of ideas just to get you started. And hopefully these ideas may even inspire you to create your own unique introduction.

Using a quotation

Quotations make good openings for several reasons: They're easy to find; they're easy to tie into your topic; and, if chosen appropriately, they make you sound smart. Whether funny or serious, they get the audience's attention.

You'll find plenty of books stuffed full of quotations. But a good place to start may be to check out a free Web site: www. quotationspage.com. You'll find quotations from all of the usual suspects, from Shakespeare to Winston Churchill, Aristotle and Oscar Wilde.

Using a rhetorical question

Asking questions is an effective way of introducing a topic. A *rhetorical question* is one that you ask but don't actually want the audience to shout out answers to. But, by giving them pause for thought, a rhetorical question involves the audience as they mentally answer.

For example, a speaker talking about the provision of health services in the developing world may ask: 'When you're thirsty, how far do you go to get a drink? Maybe you go to the kitchen tap or to the fridge for a can of your favourite soft drink. But imagine living in the developing world and having to treck a mile each way every time you want a drink. How would that make you feel?'

Using a story or anecdote

Everyone loves stories – especially if they're real, personal, and relevant.

If you're presenting on a topic, you probably have a wealth of experience about it. So take a moment to consider the right story to share with others. Remember that your own story or anecdote can appeal either to the logical or emotional needs of your audience (see Chapter 5 for more on audience needs).

Using a startling statistic

We have some good news and some bad news about statistics. The bad news is statistics tend to put people to sleep. The good news is that dramatic, carefully chosen statistics keep people *from* going to sleep. They serve as a wake-up call. A startling statistic is particularly effective in an introduction. (See the section on statistics in Chapter 8.)

A good resource for statistics is the National Statistics Web site: www.statistics.gov.uk. This site is packed with statistics covering Britain's economy, population, and society at both the national and local level – both in summary and detailed form. For example, you'll find statistics about births and deaths, economic performance of businesses, and how much people spent in shops last year. And this information's all published free of charge.

Using a startling fact

An interesting or startling fact always provides a good way to start a presentation. If you find the fact fascinating, chances are so will your audience. Counter-intuitive facts are always thought-provoking, too.

Say you're giving a talk about exercise and weight loss. One interesting fact is that people who embark on a new pro-gramme of exercise sometimes actually put on weight to begin with – because they are gaining muscle and losing fat. Muscle is a lot denser than fat, so people can actually shrink in waist size but go up in weight. This kind of slightly unexpected fact can kick off a presentation or talk very effectively.

Using an historic event

An historic event that relates to your topic is always a good way to begin a presentation. Historical references make you look smart and put your topic in perspective.

For example, say that you're giving a talk on the topic of apathy and the importance of voting in elections. Here are some interesting historical events that were determined by just a single vote:

- ✔ More than a 1,000 years ago in Greece, an entire meeting of the Church Synod was devoted to one question: Is a woman a human being or an animal? The issue was finally settled by one vote, and the consensus was that women do indeed belong to the human race. The motion passed, however, by just one vote.

- ✔ In 1776, the nascent United States of America decided by just one vote to adopt English as its national language instead of German.

- ✔ In 1923, just one vote was enough to elect the leader of a new political party in Munich. His name was Adolf Hitler.

The Internet is a great source of free historical information. For both medieval and modern British history, try the digital library at British History Online: www.british-history.ac.uk.

Using something that happened today

Any fact about the date you're speaking on can be used to open your presentation. Is it a holiday? Is it a famous person's birthday? Is it the day the light bulb was invented? This device is closely related to the historical event opening, but is not identical. You're not looking for an historic event related to your topic. You're just looking for some kind of event that occurred on this date. (When you find the event, then you relate it to your topic.)

A good place to mine for information is the 'This Day In History' section of the History Channel Web site: www.history channel.com. For example, picking April Fool's Day, the Web site tells us that the Royal Air Force was formed with the amalgamation of the Royal Flying Corps (RFC) and the Royal Naval Air Service (RNAS).

Using the title of your presentation

Many speakers use the title of their presentation as part of their introduction. For example, you may be giving a political talk entitled 'Little Trouble in Big China'. You could try to weave the title of your presentation into your introduction in the following way:

> There's a film called *Big Trouble in Little China*, but I'm here to talk about Little Trouble in Big China. Or at least that's the Chinese government's version, as they censor much of what goes out. So it seems that there is Little Trouble in Big China.

Provoking your audience

Want to get your audience's attention? Get them riled up about something as soon as you start speaking.

Here's how James P. Grant, the late Executive Director of the United Nations Children's Fund (UNICEF), used a provoking opening at an international development conference: 'Permit me to begin with a few friendly provocations: First, I would suggest that nobody – not the West, not the United States, nobody – "won the Cold War".'

Showing your knowledge of your audience

An audience is always complimented if you know something about them. This tactic shows that you made an effort to learn about the audience members. The perfect place to display this knowledge is in your introduction.

Take a look at the 'Analysing Your Audience' section in Chapter 2 to come up with some relevant information that you may be able to add to your presentation.

For example, if you're speaking at a local school, you may mention the time of year (such as start of term, end of term, impending exams, and so on). Or if you're speaking to a charity, you may refer to when they received their charter or to some snippet of information you gleaned from their Web site.

Referring to your audience immediately makes them appreciate that you've taken the time to research them rather than just delivered a standard talk or presentation.

Developing a common bond

Showing that you have something in common with the audience is always a good tactic.

For example, if you're speaking to a group of businesspeople, do you have any family members or friends that you could refer to?

My brother-in-law is an accountant. And when I first met him he went to great pains to tell me how his job isn't at all boring. And when he began to explain that his job isn't about counting beans but actually investigating how businesses make and lose money, well, I was hooked.

Emphasising the subject's importance

Of course, the topic should be of interest to the audience. But saying that something is important and explaining why gets immediate attention.

Say you're presenting at a medical conference on the topic of diseases in developing countries:

> I'd like to remind you of the importance of this issue. This is human history in the making. We have the power to eliminate tuberculosis in sub-Saharan Africa. Just think how monumental that might be – for children growing up in 10 years'

time to not have to worry about catching a disease that has been all but wiped out in the Western world.

Referring to the occasion

Want an easy way to begin? Just remind the audience of why you're speaking – the occasion that has brought you all together. And refer to the emotions or thoughts that may be going through the audience members' heads.

A scientist speaking at a climate change conference may refer specifically to the audience and other delegates:

> I think there are mixed emotions in the room. There is a genuine sense of excitement that we are all gathered here today to share our latest findings about climate change and its impact on our ecologies. But there's also a palpable sense of trepidation in the room too, as we all recognise that we are on the brink of multiple, and possibly irreversible, ecological catastrophes.

Relating your presentation to previous presentations

If you're not the first speaker of the day, you can begin by telling the audience how your presentation relates to what they've already heard. Doing so helps the audience to see the big picture and how the different speakers' topics are related.

Of course, using this tactic means getting to know beforehand what your fellow speakers are going to talk about. Otherwise you may have to come up with something on the spot – and you need a lot of practice of standing up in front of audiences to develop that skill.

A useful tool is to talk about some aspect of a previous presenter's talk that you found 'interesting'. For example: 'What was most interesting to me about the preceding sessions we've had so far today was that we hear remarkably similar things from our clients here at ABC Bank. In fact, I'd go on to say that . . .'

Chapter 7

Finishing on a High Note

. . . .

In This Chapter

▶ Making sure your conclusion works

▶ Putting together a powerful conclusion

▶ Closing with style

. . . .

Do you remember being told as a child, 'Don't start what you can't finish'? This advice goes for presentations – too many people who start them don't know how to finish them off.

The conclusion is one of the most important parts of your presentation or speech. If the introduction is your first impression, the conclusion is your last one – *and your last chance to make one*. As they go for coffee break or depart the event, your conclusion will be what sticks in your listeners' minds. And your conclusion plays a key role in determining, after days or weeks have passed, how your audience will remember you and your message.

In our model of comparing a presentation to the smooth flight of an airplane, the conclusion is the landing. The passengers – your audience – don't want the landing to be sudden or bumpy. They don't want to land in the wrong place. And most importantly, they *do* want you to land.

Making Your Conclusion Work

A cynic may say the conclusion's job is to let the audience know when to wake up. For non-cynics, the conclusion must accomplish each of the following three major functions in order to be successful:

✔ **Summarise your presentation.** The conclusion must provide a summary of your major points. This quick review should also remind the audience of your attitudes toward the ideas you've expressed. It should also show how the points relate to each other and your topic.

✔ **Provide closure.** The conclusion must give the audience a feeling that your talk is complete. People have a psychological need for closure. They want speeches and presentations to have beginnings, middles, and ends – especially ends. They don't want to be left hanging. Your conclusion must address this need.

✔ **Make a great final impression.** The conclusion is your last chance to influence audience expectations. You want to end on a high note. Go out with a bang. Leave them stamping in the aisles. (Pick your own cliché.) The conclusion should grab their attention and be as impactful as a punch to the stomach (only less painful, hopefully). It should possess an emotional appeal (see Chapter 5 for more on emotional appeals) that illuminates the compelling nature of your entire speech.

Creating the Perfect Conclusion

Remember the ending to every fairy tale you've ever heard? 'And then they lived happily ever after.' Your presentation may not have much in common with a fairy tale, but you can create a similarly perfect ending for it. The following sections give you some simple rules.

Cueing the audience in advance

The audience likes for you to let them know in advance that you plan on concluding. Tell them when you're getting *close* to your conclusion. 'Turning now to my final point' and 'I'll give two more examples before I wrap up' are types of statements that give the audience confidence that you'll reach your final destination – soon. These statements also help the audience formulate an estimated time of arrival.

Making it sound like a conclusion

People expect a conclusion to sound a certain way – like a conclusion. Audiences tend to become upset if you think you're finished but they don't. So make the wrap-up obvious. Use phrases such as 'in conclusion', 'to conclude', or 'in closing'. Such phrases are always good starting points – for ending.

Another handy tip is to write the word 'Conclusion' into any visual aids you may be using (see Chapter 10 for more on visual aids).

Finding the right length

The conclusion should usually be about 5 to 10 per cent of your speech. Your summation can be too short, but a much more common mistake is making it too long. Don't go on forever. Sum up and sit down.

Writing it out

Two reasons exist for writing out your conclusion. First, doing so combats stage fright. The period when you're concluding is the second most jittery time for speakers. (The most likely time for stage fright to strike is when you begin; see Chapter 6 for more on introductions.) If you write out the conclusion, you don't have to worry about forgetting it. Second, and more important, if you write out the conclusion, you know when to conclude. A written summation's an insurance policy to protect you from rambling.

Making the last words memorable

The last few lines of your conclusion are the most important. So make them memorable. Go for an emotional connection with the audience members. Make them laugh. Make them think. Make them stand up and applaud.

Here's a simple formula for setting up your final line: Just say, 'I have one final thought that I want to leave you with.' (An alternative is, 'If you remember just one thing I've said today, remember this . . .') Then give your audience a heck of a thought. Word that concluding thought strongly and make it relevant – to your talk and your audience.

Announcing your availability

No matter what the circumstances of your speaking engagement, always make time to answer questions after you're finished. Announce your availability during the conclusion.

Imagine you're in the audience. You hear a talk that you think is absolutely terrific. When the presentation's finished, you go to talk with the speaker, and he gives you the brush off. Blimey. First, you feel stupid. Then you get angry. And then you change your opinion of the presenter and the presentation, right? Now you think the speaker is an idiot, and the talk wasn't so great after all. So don't be an idiot. Be kind to your fans. And don't forget – the fact that you're finished speaking doesn't mean that you're done quite yet.

Avoiding common mistakes

Sometimes what you don't say in your conclusion is even more important than what you do say. Avoid the following common mistakes:

- ✔ **Going over your time limit.** Make the conclusion coincide with the end of your allotted time. If you want to be perceived as a genius, finish five minutes early, but don't go on for longer than expected. An old joke on the lecture circuit defines a 'second wind' as what a speaker gets after he or she says, 'In conclusion'. Don't let that happen to you. It's not pretty.

- ✔ **Rambling.** Reviewing the points you've already made should be done in a brief and orderly manner – preferably in the order you discussed them. Make the conclusion easy to follow. Stick to your plan.

- ✔ **Adding new points at the end.** The conclusion is a time to review what you've already said – not make another speech. Introducing new ideas in the conclusion means that you haven't properly fitted them into the overall framework of your presentation, which in turn means that these ideas will have less impact. The audience will have to figure out where they belong. And actually – the audience will just want to go home.

✔ **Saying you forgot to mention something.** Doing so makes you look disorganised, and the audience worries that you'll make another speech. One solution is: If the point is really important, boil it down to a very succinct statement. Then, after you've summarised the points you've already made, say you want to leave the audience members with one final thought. Then give them the point you forgot to mention. If you had already planned to leave them with a different final thought, don't worry. Just say you want to leave them with two final thoughts. First give the point you forgot and then give the final thought you had planned. (Yes, this is an exception to the rule against adding new points at the end.)

Wrapping It Up in Style

Psychologists have found that audiences tend to remember introductions and conclusions more strongly than what is said in the middle of a presentation. Assuming you've started with a strong introduction, don't let yourself down with a flaccid conclusion.

Referring back to the opening

If one of the functions of the conclusion is to provide closure, then referring back to your introduction is a great way to do it. You use the conclusion to return to remarks you made in your introduction. If you asked a question in your opening, you answer it in the conclusion. If you told a story, you refer to it again. This technique gives a wonderful sense of completeness to your presentation.

Using a quotation

You can never go wrong ending with an inspirational quotation related to your message. Just make sure your choice is not only inspired but also totally relevant.

Asking a question

Asking the right question can be a powerful way to end a presentation. Presumably the question implies an answer – the one you want the audience to reach.

Closed questions (those that can only be answered 'yes' or 'no') are good ways to finish off your talk. Then no one can fail to answer the question for themselves.

For example, say a doctor is talking about eating too much fat as a cause of heart disease. The doctor might finish by asking: 'Now that you've heard how we have to crack open a patient's rib cage, do you think you fancy having triple bypass surgery?'

Telling a story

You can choose from several types of stories: funny, shocking, moving, dramatic, educational, personal, fictional, biblical, or allegorical. Any one of them can be effective if appropriate for your topic and your audience.

Reciting a poem

If you recite a poem, make it short. Audiences switch off very quickly if you read more than half a dozen lines. The poem can be inspirational or funny, but it must, must, must tie into your talk. And because poetry is a pretty much neglected art form these days, you may want to get a second opinion. Share your poem with a friend or colleague and see if they get the link between it and your topic.

Telling the audience what to do

This type of ending is very specific. You conclude by telling the audience *exactly* what to do.

Say you're talking about fostering and adoption. After presenting the trials and tribulations involved in fostering and adopting, you might tell your audience exactly how they can do it: 'Find out more at the Barnardo's Web site. It's

Barnardos.org.uk and there's a very clear link to the pages about fostering and adoption. So, again, that's Barnardo's, spelt b-a-r-n-a-r-d-o-s, dot org, dot uk. Just do it.'

Asking for help

Just ask for help. This technique's a simple but overlooked conclusion. Most people really do respond. If they've taken the time to come to listen to your talk (and assuming you carried it off with panache), then your audience are more than likely to help. So whether you are looking for volunteers to help with a fund-raising 'bring and buy' sale or for business-people to donate prizes for a raffle or volunteers to contribute to an organisational change programme, just ask. You may be surprised.

Part III
Making Your Presentation or Speech Sparkle

In this part . . .

What's the difference between an average presentation or speech and a truly engaging one? Exciting words and eye-catching visual aids. And we cover these techniques in this part. In these chapters, you discover how to choose the right words and order them into powerful combinations. We also talk about how to create stunning visual aids.

Chapter 8

Making Sense of Your Presentation

*L*ife would be a lot simpler if we could sit down in just one go and dictate exactly what we wanted to say in our presentation. Unfortunately, the vast majority of people can't. So you must face the inevitable: Editing your presentation content and adding effective transitions. But don't worry. We've put together some techniques that minimise the time you spend on these chores and make them relatively pain-free. And although a shot of whiskey may have the same painless effect, our techniques for editing and adding transitions leave you with a solid presentation – instead of a hangover. (You can turn it into a great speech or presentation by reading Chapters 9 and 10.)

Editing Your Presentation – Pain-free

Just thinking of the word 'edit' may give you a headache. But just as you should never think of giving a presentation without practising it, don't think of even practising your presentation until you've edited it. Just check out the guidelines in the sections that follow. You'll find that the time you spend editing your presentation is not only painless, but also totally worth it.

Using conversational language

Failure to distinguish between oral and written language in a presentation is a common mistake. People write a presentation as though the document's a memo or a report – but a presentation must be read orally, not visually. What you write must be designed for the ear, not the eye.

When you write a presentation, some of your writing vocabulary will inevitably creep into your talk. When you edit the presentation, you must find those instances and eliminate them. Keep your language conversational.

Reading your presentation out loud

Reading your presentation aloud isn't just for practise. If you write for the ear, you need to hear what you're writing so you can edit out text that just doesn't sound right. While reading your presentation out loud, work through the following questions:

- ✔ **How does it sound?** You can't tell how a presentation works by reading it. You have to hear how it sounds. Or ask someone else to listen to it. If it doesn't sound like a presentation, which only people other than yourself can determine, you may have more work to do.

- ✔ **Does it have a good rhythm?** No, you're not writing a song, but you are creating a performance designed for the ear.

- ✔ **Can you communicate each idea without running out of breath?** Long sentences may be impressive if you're writing a dissertation but they can be tough on your lungs when you're speaking in front of an audience unless you're a swimmer or trumpet player who has mastered the art of breath control and incorporated that talent into your delivery style. Phew.

- ✔ **Have you cut out all the tongue twisters?** Words can look good on paper but be difficult to say out loud. If you find yourself stumbling over a word, change it. For example, one of us (Rob) recently had to present a theory expounded by a Russian scientist called Mikhail Csikszentimihalyi. Despite much practising, he decided to put the scientist's name into the appendices of the visual aids rather than have to say it!

✓ **Have you eliminated phrases that appear harmless on paper but are embarrassing when spoken?** For example: 'One smart fellow, he felt smart. Two smart fellows, they both felt smart. Three smart fellows, they all felt smart.' Say these lines aloud as quickly as you can a few times. You'll find out why they generate more than a few giggles in the school playground!

Keeping the language simple

Many speakers feel that they have to throw in a lot of big words to show how smart they are. Wrong. Smart speakers do just the opposite.

So avoid the big fancy words unless you feel they add something. Why use the word 'utilise' when 'use' may do just as well?

Avoiding long sentences

Brevity is the soul of understanding. No, that sentence is *not* a mistake. We know the expression is really 'Brevity is the soul of wit', but we want *you* to know that brevity also has a big impact on comprehension. The more words a sentence contains, the more difficult it is to understand. Longer sentences also tend to contain more sub-clauses that can make your audience struggle to keep up. Remember, on paper, a reader can re-read a complicated sentence – but they can't rewind your performance with quite the same ease. Look through your presentation. If you find a lot of sentences with more than 20 words, start rewriting.

Using the active voice

The active voice makes your sentences more forceful and powerful because someone is doing something in them. The passive voice sounds wimpy. A sentence in passive voice may read: 'There's a bonus given by the boss once a year.' But the same idea using the active voice reads: 'The boss gives a bonus once a year.' The passive voice is a weed that creeps into your writing – keep pruning it out.

Being specific

Writing instructors have an old saying that also applies to presentations – 'specific is terrific'. This phrase means that concrete words and examples are more effective than vague words and descriptions. Contrast 'I went to the supermarket' with 'I went to Tesco'. The word 'Tesco' is more specific than 'supermarket'. Using a specific example creates a stronger image and makes it easier for members of the audience to picture it in their heads. Or say you're describing an accident that occurred in a school playground. You could say, 'A boy ran into the wall and got hurt.' You could also say, 'A boy ran into the wall and scraped his arm in three places. The school nurse had to apply bandages to stop the bleeding.' Being specific and painting a picture in the minds of your audience can make a big difference to your presentation.

Using exciting verbs

Verbs are where the action is. So make them exciting. Let verbs help create a picture for your listeners. Say you're telling some war story from work: 'I asked Smith to give me the file.' Asked? Why not begged, pleaded, or implored? A good thesaurus can do wonders.

Of course, a thesaurus can also be used excessively. The sentence 'Run Dick run' doesn't have to become 'Dash Dick gallop'. The thesaurus should be used as a tool not an obsession. You still want to keep your language transparently unaffected. Oops, sorry, we mean simple!

Getting rid of clichés and buzzwords

'People are our most important resource.' 'We partner with our customers.' 'Think outside the box.' Stop. Give everyone a break. Instead of parroting the latest corporate clichés, come up with something fresh. Doing so gets more attention.

Avoid buzzwords, too. 'Synergy', 're-engineering', 'excellence', 'strategic' – how do you react when you hear a load of these words strung together? Do you visualise the speaker as a corporate robot and put your mind on automatic? Peppering your presentation with buzzwords invites your audience to ignore what you're saying – if they even understand it.

Occasionally a cliché or buzzword may actually fit into your message. But most of the time, these terms get used because the presenter is too lazy to think of another way to express what they really mean. So take a few moments to think about what you're really saying. Doing so's not that difficult.

Perfecting the pace

If all your sentences are the same length, you can end up sounding more like a lullaby than a presentation or talk and run the risk of lulling your audience to sleep. So vary the pace. Use short sentences and long sentences. Throw in a rhetorical question. Don't let the rhythm become monotonous.

Avoiding foreign words and phrases

So you did French at school. And you've practised and can still remember a lot of it. Good for you. But if you want to speak French, go to France. Dropping a load of foreign phrases into your talk doesn't impress anybody but you. Doing so just makes you appear pompous, and can leave your audience wondering what you just said. (Besides, English was good enough for good old William Shakespeare.)

Making Transitions

Transitions may be the most overlooked part of any presentation; yet they're one of the most important. Transitions are how you get from one point in your presentation to another. They don't involve dramatic rhetorical devices like the introduction or conclusion. They don't offer fascinating information or anecdotes like the body of the presentation. Transitions are still crucial, though – they're the glue that holds your whole presentation together.

Figuring out how to use transitions

Even if your presentation has the world's greatest introduction, body, and conclusion, you still have to get from one to the other. Step forward transitions. They connect the various parts of your presentation, and they flesh out its organisation. Transitions let your audience know when you're moving from one idea to another and how all your ideas fit together.

Most people know that transitions have two traditional functions:

- ✔ To lead from one section or idea to another.

- ✔ To provide internal summaries that let the audience know where they're at, where they've been, and where they're going in regard to the presentation.

But transitions can also be used to gain and hold audience attention.

Managing the transition mission

Transitions have a lot of work to do – especially for such an overlooked part of a presentation. The following are three important tasks that transitions can perform.

Leading from one idea to another

The primary role of the transition is to lead your listeners from one idea to another.

Perhaps the most important transition is the one between the introduction and the body of your talk. In our airplane model, this point is when the plane pulls out of the takeoff pattern and settles into cruising mode. Turbulence here can make the passengers very nervous. They want to know that the plane is heading in the right direction and that you'll provide a smooth flight all the way.

But the transitions between major points are also crucial. Speakers often get it wrong here. For example, you're sitting in the audience listening to a presentation and the speaker is talking about the monetary policy of Bolivia. But the next thing you know, the speaker is discussing a labour shortage in Eastern Europe. How did you get from Bolivia to Eastern Europe? Probably without a transition.

 Fortunately, a simple way exists to handle the transition between the introduction and body of your presentation, as well as the transitions between main points. Here's the secret: Organise your presentation around a number of points and state that number in your introduction. Then the transitions are a breeze. 'Today I will be speaking about the three reasons for the coming worldwide economic depression. First is the monetary policy of Bolivia . . . The second reason we are headed for a worldwide depression is the labour shortage in Eastern Europe . . . Third . . .' This process is transition by numbers, and it works.

 The numbering technique can also be used to make transitions to and between subpoints. 'First is the monetary policy of Bolivia. There are two aspects to Bolivian policy that are troubling . . . '

One more important transition exists: that between the body of your presentation and the conclusion. And this transition's very easy to handle. Sometimes you can just say 'In conclusion' and it works. But remember that this transition must alert the audience that you're going into your close. Use expressions such as: 'What can we learn from all this?', 'Let me leave you with one final thought', 'Now, in my three remaining minutes, let me remind you of what we've discussed'. Make the transition sound sound as though you're going to wind down and wrap up.

Summarising

The second traditional function of transitions (see the earlier section 'Leading from one idea to another' for the first) is to provide internal summaries – short announcements that let the audience know where they've been, where they are, and where they're going. The need for these summaries is frequently dismissed by inexperienced speakers who feel that they're too repetitive – that they're just filler. Well, yes and no. Internal summaries *are* repetitive, but they're *not* filler. They play a vital role in any presentation, especially those longer than a few minutes.

In understanding a presentation, speakers have a distinct advantage over the audience – they know what they're trying to say. Speakers know exactly what their message is, how it's structured, and all its points and subpoints. In writing the presentation, speakers have an opportunity to read their message many times. Audiences don't have that luxury. They only hear the presentation once – as it's given. They can't put the presentation in reverse, play it again, and freeze-frame the parts they didn't catch.

Here are a few tips about using internal summaries:

- An internal summary should succinctly state what you just covered and announce where you are in the presentation.

- Use an internal summary every time you move from one major point in your talk to another major point.

- Internal summaries can also be used when moving from subpoint to subpoint.

- The longer your presentation, the more internal summaries you need.

Getting attention

Transitions can also be used to gain attention. Although they're not traditionally used for this purpose, no reason exists why they shouldn't be. Under a more traditional view, transitions can serve as internal summaries telling your audience where they've been, where they are, and where they're going. The *where they're going* part raises interesting possibilities for gaining attention.

When you tell your audience where they're going, why not make it exciting? Instead of just restating the structure of your talk in a straightforward, matter-of-fact manner, why not try to inject a little something different into the proceedings? Use a *teaser.* A teaser is the short blurb you hear on some radio and television programmes just before they go to a commercial break. For example, 'Coming up in the next half of our show: our househunters discover that their property isn't all they thought it was' or 'A politician who *kept* a promise – right after these announcements'. The teaser is designed specifically to get your attention and keep you from changing the channel.

You can use the teaser technique to make your internal summaries excite the audience members about what lies ahead in your presentation. Give them some great coming attractions that keep them glued to their seats. How do you do that? Think about why the audience should even listen to your talk. What's in it for them? As you write your transitions about what's coming up, frame them in terms of audience benefits.

Avoiding common transition mistakes

Transitions form the glue that holds a presentation together. Unfortunately, many speakers become unglued trying to insert transitions properly. Avoid the following mistakes.

Too few

Not having enough transitions in your presentation is the biggest mistake. Having more can't hurt because you can never make your presentation too clear to your audience. You've been living with your presentation for quite a while. You're intimately familiar with the content; your audience isn't. The more guidance you can give the audience about how your presentation's structured and where it's going, the better.

Too brief

If the transition is too brief, your audience can easily miss it. Missing it may have the same effect as having no transition at all. The most common, and overused, brief transition is 'and'. We've heard talks that used 'and' almost exclusively as a transition and the effect is almost comical. The presentation sounds like a load of disjointed ideas tacked together – 'and' is the tack. 'In addition' is a close runner-up.

Too similar

Variety is the spice of life – and it also works wonders with transitions. Don't use the same couple of transitional phrases over and over again. Doing so gets boring. Use an assortment of transitions: 'Now let's take a look at . . .', 'In addition . . .', 'The next point is . . .', 'For example . . .', and 'By that I mean . . .'. Endless possibilities exist.

Chapter 9

Getting the Words Right

● ●

In This Chapter

▶ Choosing words to create a powerful message

▶ Developing a catch phrase

▶ Using rhetorical devices

● ●

*O*ver 10,000 useless words exist in the English language, apparently, and a great many of them come in handy for writing computer manuals and political speeches. Some of these words may even come in handy for *your* speeches and presentations – depending on what you want to accomplish. Whatever your goal, you can't escape the fact that words are the basic building blocks of a good presentation or speech. If you want to be a successful public speaker, you have to get the words right, and this chapter shows you how.

Honing Your Tone and Style

We'll start with a cautionary tale. A (nameless) politician used to speak on the topic of overly generous state benefits. His booming voice thundered across the room, 'From NHS costs of prenatal care to pension benefits, the government is taking care of people from womb to tomb.' The rhyming words of 'womb' and 'tomb' gave the line a nice ring and always got applause. But the politician got bored with the line, so he introduced a new version during a luncheon speech to a women's political association. Instead of 'womb to tomb', he said he was sick of the government taking care of people from 'sperm to worm'. The audience silence was deafening.

What can we learn from this story? Three things: Don't talk about sperm to a women's political association. Don't talk about worms while people are eating. And don't forget that tone and style are important – they have a major effect on how your ideas are received.

Choosing the right words

Imagine you're thinking about buying a new car. The salesperson says: 'This is a nice car with agreeable handling and good acceleration.' Hmm. You're not sure if those words are really selling the car. But consider: 'This is an exceptional car with fantastic handling and breath-taking acceleration.' Which version do you think paints the more evocative picture?

'Breath-taking', 'fantastic', and 'exceptional' are colourful words. They are more graphic than mundane descriptive words such as 'nice' and 'good'.

Certain words grab attention without really saying anything. If someone says, 'This is an urgent matter' or 'This is really important', they've said nothing to you, but they've still got your attention. Which is what these words do: Grab attention without giving away what you want to talk about. To maintain an audience's attention throughout your presentation, scatter a few carefully chosen words such as 'urgent', 'important', and 'critical' to flag up your key points.

While certain words are more colourful and expressive, be careful not to overuse them. If every other word is 'outstanding', 'compelling', 'exciting', 'perfect', and so on, your audience will switch off. Colourful words lose their power to make an audience sit up and take notice if they're overused.

Figuring out how to use jargon

Real mode device drivers are fine, as long as you hook them up to a hybrid 16/32 bit OS and retain control of the configuration of the SNMP agent and log-on domains. Okay, right, this line makes perfect sense, doesn't it? Er, no. Using your own jargon in presentations is usually summed up in two words – avoid it. Jargon is often incomprehensible and using it creates a barrier between you and your audience. However, if you explain your jargon – educate your audience as to its meaning – you shouldn't have a problem using it.

Jargon can sometimes create a bond. In order to explain why, we need to introduce an academic concept: The inclusionary and exclusionary functions of language. The concept sounds complicated but really isn't: It simply means that one of the ways that groups of people define themselves is through the use of language, and breaking through some of this jargon is like finding out a secret password. If you speak the language, you're in (or *included*); if you don't speak it, you're out (or *excluded*). Jargon is the language unique to each group.

Jargon is so widespread because every group creates its own jargon as a way of defining its membership. Each trade and profession has its own jargon. Many organisations have their own jargon. The finance team may use very different jargon from the human resources people or the sales division. Clubs and associations have their own jargon. Even individual families have their own jargon.

So what does use of jargon mean for presentations? Plenty. Are you an outsider in relation to the group you're addressing? You can create rapport with the audience by using some of their jargon in your talk. Doing so is relatively easy, and demonstrates that you made an effort to learn about the audience. Using their jargon also suggests that you understand something about the audience. Talking to surgeons? Find out what a 'lap chole' is and refer to it in your presentation. Talking to estate agents? Find out what 'FSBO' means and drop it into your talk. (For more on finding out what might be appropriate jargon, see Chapter 3.)

Creating Catch Phrases

The *catch phrase* provides a tried-and-true method for drawing attention to a key point and helping audiences remember it. Just turn on your radio or TV for some examples – the adverts are full of catch phrases: 'Because you're worth it', 'I'm loving it', and 'Va va voom'. These phrases 'catch' in your memory – which is what they're designed to do. Every time you think about a catch phrase, you automatically think about the associated product and its key sales point. Constant repetition of the phrase by those cunning advertisers augments this effect.

The catch phrase technique isn't limited to advertising. Anyone can use it in any type of presentation or speech. Just pick an important point, build a catch phrase around it, and repeat it throughout your presentation.

Spicing Up Your Speech with Classic Rhetorical Devices

If you had a dispute in ancient Greece, you faced both good and bad news. The good news: Lawyers weren't invented. The bad news: You had to argue your own case. The ancient Greeks developed all sorts of rhetorical devices to improve their speeches – because they wanted to win.

This section presents a few of the classic devices. And don't worry, they still work today. Anyone from 6-year-olds to lawyers to professional speakers still use these techniques, and use them effectively.

Hyperbole

Hyperbole is a fancy word for exaggeration. People use hyperbole instinctively in everyday conversation: 'I was waiting a year for you to get off the phone.' 'It's about a million miles from here to Hong Kong.' Hyperbole's a wonderful device for emphasising a point in a speech or presentation. Here's an example from a comedian describing his early days:

> One of the first clubs I performed at was a small, dark place. It was so dark I could barely see the three people in the room – the two in the front row listening to me and the guy in the back row developing film.

Allusion

An *allusion* is a reference to a person, object, or event from the Bible, mythology, or literature. Here are a couple of examples:

> ✔ Allowing children to drink alcohol from the age of 16
> would be like opening a Pandora's box of trouble ranging
> from early liver damage to alcoholism.
>
> ✔ Every organisation has an Achilles' heel – a weakness
> that we can exploit. We just need to find out what it is.

Alliteration

Alliteration refers to a phrase in which the words begin with
the same sound. For example, the phrase 'salacious, sleazy
scandal' uses the repetition of the 's' at the beginning of each
word to create a memorable sound.

You can also use alliteration to make the title of your talk
more memorable. For example, the title 'Persecuted People in
Politics' may be easier to recall than 'Persecuted Individuals
and Government'.

Metaphor

A *metaphor* is a short, implied comparison that transfers the
properties of one item to another. A classic example comes
from Martin Luther King's 'I Have a Dream' speech in which he
talks about: '. . . the manacles of segregation and the chain of
discrimination.'

The metaphor can add a poetic quality to your speech while
still allowing you to make a point. Say you want to talk about
the devastation caused by a natural disaster. Rather than
referring to the hurricane, you can dress it up in a metaphor:
'An invisible hand decimated the village.'

Simile

A *simile* is like a metaphor except that you make a directly
stated comparison of one thing to another. (A simile usually
uses the words 'like' or 'as' to make the comparison.)

Say, for example, a politician is talking about the need to
control unscrupulous financial advisors: 'You have a massive
influx of inexperienced investors, and a real potential for

conflicts of interest – it's like dry kindling and a match. And it's something I want to avoid as I've seen too many people's life savings go up in smoke.'

Comedy writer Ben Elton uses a pattern whereby he confounds our expectations of a simile: 'In my hallway, there sat a big square box, which was exactly like . . . a big, square box.' The audience is then surprised by the unexpected.

Rhetorical question

A *rhetorical question* refers to a question that the speaker asks for effect. The audience isn't expected to answer. Rhetorical questions are designed to focus attention on the subject of the question. This device is often used in introductions, conclusions, or transitions.

For example, say you want to highlight the plight of abandoned dogs:

> How would you feel if you were thrown out onto the street? Would you enjoy being cold and lonely? Would you enjoy scrabbling around in dustbins for a bite to eat? Would you be content and happy? Would you?

The rule of three

The *rule of three* refers to the technique of grouping together three words, phrases, or sentences. For some reason, a grouping of three items makes a powerful impression on the human mind. (Don't ask us why. Just trust us that it does.)

Some of the most famous passages from the world's greatest oratory have used this technique:

- ✔ 'I came. I saw. I conquered.' (Julius Caesar)
- ✔ '. . . government of the people, by the people, for the people . . .' (Abraham Lincoln)

Business speakers frequently use this technique. The beauty of the rule of three is that it can work its magic on any topic – no matter how commonplace or mundane. Just take a few minutes to think about your subject. You can always come up with three items to group together. Are you talking about a new accounting procedure that must be followed by all employees? It affects managers, hourly staff, and temps. Is your subject quality management? It starts with awareness, training, and commitment.

Repetition

Repetition refers to repeating a group of words in an identical rhythm. This device draws attention to the phrase and can even be used to pull a whole speech together. Martin Luther King's 'I Have a Dream' speech is a classic example. Dr King repeated the phrase 'I have a dream' throughout his entire speech.

But repetition doesn't have to run throughout an entire presentation. You can use the technique to dramatise one section, or even one sentence, of your talk. The following example uses repetition to stress the effects of global warming on our children's future:

> It's our children who will suffer if we don't do something about global warming. It's our children who will see the seas rise and overwhelm their homes. It's our children who will ask us why we did nothing.

So repetition is a dramatic way to create a rhythm, to make a point, or to show your style. Repetition's a dramatic way to be dramatic.

Chapter 10

Developing Great Visual Aids

*Y*ou've heard the saying, 'A picture's worth a thousand words'. If that saying were literally true, then the average 20-minute presentation could be reduced to two overheads, and we'd only need to spend 40 seconds looking at them before we could all go home. But of course the reality doesn't quite work that way. A picture is worth a thousand words only under certain circumstances. This chapter explores the nature of those circumstances – when visual aids help, when visual aids hinder, and what visual aids can really do for you – get the picture?

Using Charts and Graphs

Charts and graphs are commonly used to depict numerical data. They're also useful for expressing non-numerical relationships such as organisational structure, procedures, and lines of authority. Although charts and graphs appear most often onoverheads and PowerPoint slides, they're becoming increasingly easy to print out in hard copy form for placement on an easel or flipchart stand.

Choosing a type of chart or graph

The following points list some of the most common types of charts and graphs and how you may want to use them:

- ✔ **Bar graphs:** These are handy for comparing all kinds of data – sales of widgets versus gadgets, defect totals under various quality management programmes, drug reactions in infants versus adults.

- ✔ **Flow charts:** These are good for depicting any series of steps – company procedures, how a bill becomes a law, the pathway that an emergency phone call has to make to get through to the right service.

- ✔ **Line graphs:** These are great for showing changes over a period of time. Any kind of trend data works well – share prices, voting patterns, productivity gains.

- ✔ **Organisation charts:** Who reports to whom? What's the exact relationship between the telecommunications department and the information services department? Is the French operation an independent unit or part of the main plc? These types of questions can be answered with organisation charts.

- ✔ **Pie charts:** These are good for showing percentages in relation to each other. (The west of England region generated 7 per cent of the revenue; the east 10 per cent; the south 80 per cent; and the north 3 per cent.)

- ✔ **Tables of numerical data:** This is your basic spreadsheet layout. The format's boring, but sometimes the numbers are so dramatic that the format doesn't matter. ('As you can see from the numbers in column three, half of you are going to be made redundant next week. Surprise!')

Making effective charts and graphs

The following are a few tips to keep in mind when you're using a chart or graph:

✔ **Limit the data.** If you include too many items on a chart or graph, you make it more difficult to understand. If you have a lot of items that must be represented, rethink the graph. Maybe you can split the data into several graphs.

✔ **Size pie slices accurately.** The audience gets confused when you show a pie chart with a slice labeled '10 per cent' that looks like a quarter of the pie. If you use a pie chart, make sure the slices of the pie correspond to the real numbers.

✔ **Make absolutely sure that the numbers are correct.** Check the numbers. Recheck them. And check them again. Correct data is a credibility issue. Someone in the audience is bound to be a stickler for detail and is certain to point the error out to the entire roomful of people. If one number is incorrect, it can undermine your entire presentation.

✔ **Avoid three-dimensional bars.** Don't make bar charts with three-dimensional bars. Because it's often difficult to figure out where the bars end, the audience may not know what the numbers represent. If in doubt, keep it simple.

Making Use of PowerPoint and Overheads

You can't attend a business presentation these days without tripping over projector and computer wires. This section ensures that your audience doesn't trip over your visual aids.

Using PowerPoint

Perhaps the greatest public speaking innovation in the past couple of decades, PowerPoint has grown rapidly from a novelty to a standard. Business speakers have treated it like the greatest thing since sliced bread (or the microphone). And many people now feel unable to speak without an accompanying PowerPoint presentation.

That reliance on PowerPoint is, of course, the problem. Although PowerPoint is undoubtedly a fabulous visual aid, the medium is often treated like an abused miracle drug. People overuse it, use it improperly, or become addicted to it. Because of this abuse, PowerPoint has spawned the following three major, negative side effects:

- **The presentation is underdeveloped.** Many speakers now spend more time preparing their PowerPoint slides than what they plan to say. They think that PowerPoint *is* their presentation. It's not! You still need a compelling message with an introduction and conclusion in order to hold the attention of an audience. Throwing up a load of PowerPoint slides isn't a presentation.

- **The speaker doesn't connect with the audience.** Ever heard speakers read their speech word-for-word from their PowerPoint slides? A presentation doesn't get much more boring than that. The audience can read the slides, too. So, if you plan on just reading the slide, you may as well not show up and just send the PowerPoint presentation for the audience to read themselves. Make sure you have something that is not written up on the PowerPoint slides to say to add colour to the presentation.

- **The message is lost.** While PowerPoint can add sparkle to a presentation, it can also overwhelm your message. Be careful not to animate every single slide, add too many graphics, or have too much text popping up all over the place. Your message disappears in the gimmickry.

Fortunately, the first two PowerPoint problems are easily solved just by being aware of them. That means the next time you are giving a presentation, remember to prepare an actual speech. PowerPoint should support your material, not replace it. Remember also to talk to your audience – not read slides to them. The third problem, of losing your message, can also be easily avoided. Just follow the advice in the section 'Discovering simple design rules'.

Using overhead transparencies

Overhead transparencies are useful because you can project them without turning down the room lights. (So the audience isn't invited to snooze.) You can also write notes to yourself on the cardboard frames around the transparencies. And most important, you can reorder them as you speak.

However, overheads don't work well for a large audience because not everyone can see them clearly.

Discovering simple design rules

Whether you're using overhead transparencies or PowerPoint slides, a few basic design rules can ensure you leave your audience dazzled not dazed. Just keep the following in mind:

- ✔ **Check for spelling mistakes.** Nothing is more embarrassing than a typo projected onto a large screen. So make absolutely sure that you eliminate all the spelling mistakes from your slides and overheads. With dictionary functions on most word-processing packages, you really have no excuse not to.

- ✔ **Use relevant graphics.** Graphics are good, but only if they support a point. Too many speakers use graphics just to fill space or because they look pretty. Big mistake. If the image doesn't relate to one of the points on your slide, don't use it.

- ✔ **Be consistent.** Visually, being consistent is very important. It shows that you're organized. Don't mix and match slides or overheads from different presentations if they have different fonts, colours, or design styles. Using a mix of styles and designs is jarring, and it distracts the audience from your message.

- ✔ **Take advantage of templates.** Many software programs for creating slides and overheads include predesigned templates. You just choose a style, and the program cranks out all your slides in that design.

- ✔ **Keep the text style simple.** Many speakers feel compelled to 'pretty up' their visuals with fancy text. Don't fall prey to this temptation; too much detail makes your slides and overheads difficult to read.

- ✔ **Use builds.** A *build* is a series of slides or overheads in which each successive slide contains the bullet points from the preceding slides plus a new bullet point. Builds have become a standard part of business presentations.

Builds provide a good way to emphasise key points. The downside is that you need more slides. For example, say you want to make six points. You can put all six points on one slide. Or you can do them as a build, which means using six slides.

Using builds for more than just key points can result in overkill.

✔ **Keep the use of your logo to a minimum.** A logo should simply be a little element that says this is a presentation from your company or organisation. If you're going to put a logo on every slide, keep it small and tuck it away fairly discreetly into a corner somewhere. Otherwise it may distract from your message.

✔ **Use a mixture of uppercase or lowercase text.** Varying cases makes your overheads or slides easier for the audience to read. Using all uppercase text may be acceptable for headings or subheadings, but don't use it for the body of the text.

✔ **Use fewer rather than more words.** A common mistake is to put too much text on a slide or overhead. You don't have to include every word that you're going to say – and you shouldn't. The audience won't read all of the text and it makes you appear amateurish. Instead, just use key words or phrases that outline your ideas. Some designers refer to this as the 4 x 4 rule: Don't put more than four lines on a slide or four words in a line. Other authorities place the numbers as 6 x 6. Of course, you can exceed these guidelines, but only if you're certain that your presentation still looks coherent.

✔ **Use only two different fonts.** Using more than two fonts gives your slides a cluttered look. But an exception exists: Overheads or slides that display a logo, product name, or similar item identified by a specific font. Those items don't count toward your limit of two fonts.

✔ **Emphasise major points – not everything.** Have you ever seen students using a yellow highlighter pen to mark up 95 per cent of every page in a textbook? What are they trying to emphasise – the stuff that's not highlighted? If you want to visually direct attention to certain points, go ahead. But don't dilute your message by emphasising too much.

✔ **Use a maximum of four colours per visual.** At most, allow yourself one colour for the background, another colour for headlines, yet another colour for body text, and perhaps a fourth colour for emphasis. However, many people use fewer colours to create a sleeker, more coherent look. So remember that four colours is the absolute maximum – and not what you should automatically aim for. (You can make an exception for graphs and complex images because you may need more colours to make a pie chart or line graph understandable.)

✔ **The colours on your computer screen may look different from the colours on your overheads.** The colours you see on your computer monitor aren't always going to be the exact colours that appear on your overheads or any printouts you do of your PowerPoint presentation. Colours have a tendency to appear slightly differently depending on the brightness of a projector, the colour of the background you project on, and so on. If you're concerned about the colours, run samples to check out how they look.

Flipping for Flipcharts

A flipchart is a very large pad of paper that sits on an easel (more commonly known as the flipchart stand). Flipcharts are very common at business meetings – and for good reason. The flipchart is a very versatile visual aid. You can write on it as you speak or have pages prepared in advance. A flipchart's easy to use, too. You don't have to find any on/off switches, electrical outlets, or replacements for burned out light bulbs. A flipchart always operates properly (unless your magic marker goes dry) and is easy to transport. This business tool's also very inexpensive. However, flipcharts aren't really effective for audiences larger than 40 to 50 people. The people seated toward the back can't see what's on the chart, and many presenters misuse flipcharts so badly that even people in the front row can't decipher what the chart is supposed to say. If you plan on using a flipchart in your next presentation, check out the sections below so you can use this versatile tool properly.

Avoiding common flipchart mistakes

To make sure you avoid common flipchart mistakes, follow these guidelines:

- ✔ **Use as few words as possible.** We've seen flipcharts covered with writing from top to bottom. The paper looks like a cave wall crammed with hieroglyphics, and the text's about as easy to read as a cave wall, too. So do your audience a favour and leave some white space.

- ✔ **Write on the top two-thirds of the sheet.** Doing so makes the text easier for the audience to see. More important, by not writing on the bottom you don't have to bend down and give the audience a view of *your* bottom.

- ✔ **Write with large letters and plenty of space.** Maybe some people in your audience can read the bottom line of an eye chart, but testing them isn't your job. Make your letters large enough so that they can be read easily from the back of the room, and leave a couple of inches between lines.

- ✔ **Use a thick pen.** Even when the letters are large, they can be difficult to see if they're written in biro. So don't write using letters that look like stick figures. Use a thick-nibbed marker pen so that your letters can be read easily from the back of the room.

- ✔ **Use colours people can see easily.** Something about flipcharts brings out the artist in speakers. Control the urge. Don't use a magenta marker to write notes on the flipchart. Yellow, pink, and orange are also bad because they don't stand out enough from the white paper. In fact, if you want to make sure that your audience can see what you're writing, stick with black or blue. Those two colours can always be seen from the back of the room. The occasional bit of red for emphasis may be okay, too.

- ✔ **Use just two colours.** A rainbow is nice to look at in the sky, but not on a flipchart. You can use a few different colours to highlight various points and add emphasis. But if you use too many colours, they lose their impact and become distracting. Stick to either blue or black for your main text, and perhaps red or one other colour for titles or key words.

Using flipcharts effectively

Want to turn your flipchart into a powerful presentation tool? Try these tips that separate the masters from the disasters:

- ✔ **Use flipcharts with paper divided into small squares.** Each page should look like a piece of graph paper. The advantage is that you can use the boxes as a guide when you write. That way you know your writing will be large enough to see. The boxes can also help you keep your writing evenly spaced.

- ✔ **Correct mistakes with correction fluid.** Have you ever spent a lot of time preparing a very detailed page in your flipchart presentation only to make a minor mistake when you were just about done? Don't pull out your hair and *don't* throw away the page. Put some correction fluid over the mistake just like you would on a sheet of printer paper. Then make your correction. No one in the audience will be able to see it.

- ✔ **Write secret notes on the flipchart pages.** If you're worried that you'll forget to discuss important points, use your flipchart pages as cheat sheets. Lightly pencil in a few key words or phrases on the appropriate page. No one in the audience will be able to see your notes. This technique can also improve the text and drawings that you do want the audience to view. If you need to write or draw something as you speak, draw it lightly in pencil beforehand. When you come to that point in your talk, you can just trace over it with a marker. The outcome will look a lot better than if you start it from scratch while you're speaking.

- ✔ **Copy pictures from colouring-in books.** If appropriate, drawing simple pictures can add a lot of interest to your flipcharts. If you can't draw, use children's colouring-in books because they have simple drawings that are easy to copy and modify.

- ✔ **Use human figures.** If you're drawing pictures on your flipcharts, use human figures whenever possible. People respond to humans. (We're a narcissistic species.)

✔ **Leave a blank sheet between each sheet you use.** If you prepare your flipchart in advance, don't use every page. The paper is so thin that the audience can see through to the next sheet. So leave a blank sheet between each page that you use. Doing so also gives you room to manoeuvre if you need to add some content suddenly.

✔ **Save your flipchart pages.** You put a lot of work into the ones you prepare in advance. So use them again. If you've torn them off the flipchart, don't worry. You can tape the pages up on a wall when you reuse them. No rule exists that the sheets have to be on a flipchart stand.

Creating Great Video (and Audio)

Video is a very powerful, yet overlooked, visual aid. Today's audiences are supposed to have a short attention span due to the influence of television. So why not capture what little attention they possess with the medium they love – video? This section also discusses how to use audio to break through the attention barrier. (Although audio isn't technically a visual aid, it can create pictures *in your mind*.)

Using video

Video is so powerful that it should only be used in small doses or it may take over your presentation. A video clip can make the non-video portions – you talking – seem boring by comparison, which is exactly what you *don't* want.

Use video clips in short bursts to emphasise key points and heighten audience interest. If you're speaking to a small group, bring a video player and a TV monitor. Or most laptops these days have built-in DVD players. You can work them like an overhead projector, turning them on and off when appropriate. If you're speaking to a large audience, you need to arrange for the video to be projected onto a large screen. (That task may require some professional help.)

Using testimonials

No matter what you're selling – yourself, your ideas, or your products – you'll be hard pressed to top the persuasive power of third-party credibility. Suppose that we're going to give you a sales presentation. Hearing about the greatness of our products from some of our customers is much more persuasive than hearing it from us. Unfortunately, they usually have better things to do than accompany us on sales calls. (Video comes in here. You can videotape a customer or client singing your praises and show it to your audience.)

Tapping into other video ideas

When commercial television first took root in the 1940s, one Hollywood executive reportedly said that TV wouldn't last more than six months – people would get tired of staring at a box. He didn't realise that television then video would evolve into a wide variety of imaginative forms – all of which are designed to capture audience attention. Unless you're an imagination-impaired Hollywood executive, you should be able to work video into your presentation in lots of clever ways. Try these options:

- **Television adverts:** We once saw someone give a presentation about creativity. The speaker talked about different types of creativity and various techniques for being creative, and he illustrated the techniques with TV ads. (We assume he obtained permission to show them – see the section 'Getting permission to use content;, later in this chapter.) The audience loved watching the ads (they were very funny) and they did a good job of bringing home the points about creativity. The speaker appropriately spaced the adverts throughout his presentation and they helped maintain audience interest and energy till the end of the talk. Given the range of subject matter covered in TV ads, you can probably find one or two (hundred) that can illustrate some points in your next presentation.

- **Filmed vignettes:** A speaker made a speech about cross-cultural communication. He emphasised how Brits could avoid gaffes when doing business with people from other countries. He covered the usual stuff, but he made his message more interesting by introducing each segment with a short video. Actors, portraying businesspeople from the UK and another country, acted out a brief scene of a business meeting. The actor portraying the Brit would make every gaffe possible. The audience responded with laughter to each gaffe. So the videos were entertaining, as well as educational.

✔ **Person-on-the-street interviews:** We've seen these used for comic relief in various types of presentations. You ask a four-year-old what he or she thinks the CEO of your company does all day and videotape the answer. Or you ask people at a trade show unrelated to your industry (gourmet coffees) what they think of your latest product (a hydraulic pump). Or you ask people in your organisation to sing happy birthday to someone. You get the idea.

If you plan to use clips from television shows, films, or adverts, you must first obtain the appropriate permissions. (See 'Getting permission to use content' later in this chapter.) Of course, you could always just try to 'get away with it' – but don't say that we didn't warn you!

Including audio in your presentations

Music and sound effects can greatly enhance your presentation or speech, no matter what you're discussing. They can energise your audience, set a mood, and emphasise a point. Consider these ideas:

✔ **Set the mood with music.** Audience members are walking into the room where they'll hear you give a presentation. You have a choice. You can arrange for them to hear the theme from *Rocky* as they enter. Or they can hear nothing. Do you think it makes any difference? Yes, it does. If you play the theme from *Rocky*, your audience will get pumped up and energised (and perhaps laugh a bit at your cheesiness). Do you want your audience in a contemplative mood? Try some new age, cosmic music. Want them inflamed with patriotism? Play the National Anthem. Music can provide a wonderful warm-up act if used appropriately. Take advantage of it.

✔ **Add a beat to PowerPoint presentations.** People love to look at themselves. Meetings and conferences taking place over a couple of days often conclude with slide shows of photos taken earlier in the meeting for just this reason. (The meeting participants see themselves arriving, attending sessions, partying, and so on.) These PowerPoint shows are inevitably accompanied by loud music with a heavy bass beat (disco music is popular) because it generates energy and enthusiasm. The music makes the slide show come alive. (The slides seem to synchronise with the beat of the music.) You can adapt this technique to your own presentations. Are you giving a talk about the completion of some project (completion of a new building, graduation from school or a course, release of a new product, and so on)? Do you have photos documenting the project's progress? Put together a short PowerPoint show and add some music. Doing so's simple and very effective.

✔ **Fill time when people are thinking or writing.** Do you have a spot in your presentation when everything comes to a halt? Maybe you ask the audience to do some exercise in which they have to think about something or to take a few minutes to write something. You stop talking and silence fills the room. The silence can become oppressive after a while, and it definitely lowers the energy level of your audience. A simple solution is to play some music during this interlude. (Whatever you feel is appropriate.) Music helps maintain a minimal energy level and is also appreciated by audience members who finish early. They'll have something to listen to while the rest of the crowd finish.

Making an Impact with Multimedia

Multimedia refers to the combination of video, text, graphics, and sound. In this section, we provide a quick overview of how you can enhance your presentations and public speaking with multimedia. And we give you a few easy-to-use techniques. But this section definitely does *not* provide in-depth coverage. (See *Multimedia and CD-ROMs For Dummies* by Andy Rathbone or *PowerPoint 2003 For Dummies* by Doug Lowe, both from Wiley, for an extensive discussion of this topic.)

Getting the right multimedia equipment

You need three basic types of equipment to stage a multimedia presentation: A computer, an input device, and a projector. You also need software (see the section 'Using software for multimedia presentations' later in this chapter). You also need some kind of audio set-up.

Computers

Computers are so fast and affordable these days that you don't need to spend thousands of pounds. Amazingly, you can pick up a great laptop that will do all the multimedia you're likely to need for around £500. Any computer built in the last three years will have a sound card, a video card, and a CD-ROM/DVD drive. But if you want to get fancy with video, then you may need a video capture card to record and digitise video from television, video tapes, and camcorders.

Input devices

Input devices allow you to get sound and images into your computer in a digitised format – everything from music and video images to photographs and business cards.

- ✔ **Images:** Still images, such as slides and photographs, can be input to your computer from a digital camera or scanner. Moving images can be transferred from a video tape or camcorder with a cable you can find at any decent electronics goods store.

- ✔ **Sound:** The cables you get for video also usually work with audio devices – such as a cassette player, CD player, stereo, or radio. You run a cable from the 'headphone out' jack directly to the 'audio in' jack on your computer's sound card. Or plug in a microphone and record interviews or voiceovers directly in digitised form.

Projectors

You also need hardware that projects the sound and images of your multimedia presentation. The sound part is easy. If the room where you're speaking has a sound system, you can just plug your computer into that system. If the room doesn't contain a sound system, you may have to bring your own speakers. For image projection, you need an LCD projector. This is a special projector that allows anything displayed on your computer screen to be projected onto a large screen or wall. The latest-and-greatest models are small enough for easy portability and bright enough that room lights don't have to be turned off. (They may need to be dimmed.) Most LCD projectors also have an input for video directly from a video player – although you don't really want to fiddle with both a video player and a computer, especially as most computers have DVD drives nowadays.

Using software for multimedia presentations

The basic software requirements are Windows and Video for Windows or Windows Movie Maker. Beyond that, you need software to develop the individual pieces of your presentation and authoring software to put it all together.

Creating and editing images, sound, and text

Your first task is to construct the various images, video clips, audio clips, and slides that will make up your presentation. The following list shows you the software you need:

- ✔ **Graphics:** Graphics software ranges from simple tools, such as Paintbrush (which comes with every copy of Windows), to high-powered packages such as Photoshop and CorelDRAW!. Two of the more popular programs for image creation are Persuasion and PowerPoint. Both offer lots of help for the nonprofessional designer – so your slides won't end up with words written in 12 different fonts and 8 different colours.

- ✔ **Audio and video:** You also need special software for capturing and editing the audio and video clips that you want to use in your presentation. Almost any sound card or video capture card comes with recording and editing software that covers your basic needs. Adobe's Premier is among the better-known software products for editing video clips.

- ✔ **Text:** Most word-processing packages are capable of tagging your word-processing files for multimedia access. Your multimedia-authoring tool determines how this should be accomplished.

Authoring systems

After you assemble the various pieces of your multimedia presentation, you need a method of putting them all together and controlling them. Software known as an *authoring system* performs that function. It allows you to choreograph all the other programs – sound, video, graphics – into a coherent presentation. One of the more popular systems is Macromedia Director MX.

If using an authoring program is too much of a challenge (they do take some time and effort to learn), don't worry. Use PowerPoint or any similar program. Many people use PowerPoint to make and show slide presentations. But adding sound and videos is very easy. (See *PowerPoint 2003 For Dummies* for more help.)

Getting permission to use content

The good news about multimedia presentations is that you *can* use text, graphics, video, and audio. The bad news is that you need the rights to use that stuff.

A widespread misconception exists that you can use anything you want in a multimedia presentation. People tape stuff off the telly, capturing video clips of news items, sports events, and scenes from their favourite films. They record audio clips of music from CDs or the radio. They digitise photos and images found in books and magazines. Technically those activities are known as *copyright infringement* – an illegal activity punishable by fines and imprisonment.

So where can you get the materials you need for a multimedia presentation? Remember these two magic words – *public domain*. When an item is in the public domain, anyone is allowed to use it. No permission is required. Alternatively, just get a cassette recorder or camcorder and create your own audio and video.

Wowing Your Audience with Simple Multimedia Techniques

To get started fast, try one of these three easy suggestions. They'll knock the socks off your audience (assuming that your audience wears socks).

- ✔ **Use a testimonial from someone in your audience:** Video- or audiotape people from the organisation that you'll be addressing. Then include the clip in your presentation. Nothing is more impressive to a group than suddenly seeing one of their own members talk about how great you are.

- ✔ **Throw in a clip or image of something that just happened:** If you're speaking at an event, get there a few hours early, record people on audio or video, and work them into your presentation.

- ✔ **Use a customised effect:** The speed with which you can change a multimedia presentation creates one of its biggest advantages – you can customise it really easily. Put in as many images and audio and video files related to the audience as you can. Are you talking to car dealers? Scan in some pictures of cars.

Get a business card from someone in the company that you'll be addressing and scan in his company's logo. Then you can make it appear in the corner of every screen with your own logo. Customise as much as possible.

Being Handy with Handouts

Just as kids like to have little goodie bags to take away with them after they've been to a friend's birthday party, the members of your audience would probably like something to take away, too. When you make a presentation, bear in mind that your audience may want handouts. Consider the following things when you prepare and distribute handouts.

Making an impact with handouts

If you're going to make handouts, make them look good. Creating effective handouts isn't hard to do. Desktop-publishing programs give you lots of options for making your handouts look professional. Reproduce them on good quality paper. If you can afford it, put the handouts in a binder. Everyone likes to receive handouts. But giving out a few good-looking ones is better than a lot of hard-to-read, poorly designed ones. Remember, the handouts represent *you*.

Including the right information

Are you using PowerPoint slides or overheads in your presentation? Your audience would probably appreciate hard copies of them. Put some copies in the handouts. (If you don't, you inevitably receive requests for them.) Reprints of relevant articles, by you or others, are always popular items. Checklists are also very good. Your audience also wants to be able to contact you, so make sure you include your phone number, address, or e-mail.

Generally, if you provide more contact information, your audience will appreciate your handouts more. If you recommend products or services, talk about sources of information for a particular topic, or discuss getting in touch with an MP or a local councillor to voice concern about some issue, include lists of contact names and numbers.

Knowing when to give them out

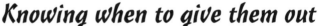

Never give out handouts before you speak. They distract the audience, and people read them instead of listening to you.

The appropriate time to distribute handouts depends on their function. If the handouts summarise your points and present supplemental information, then distribute them *after* your talk. But if your handouts include audience participation exercises or other materials that you want to refer to while you're speaking, give them out *before* you begin. Handouts distributed before you speak can also encourage the audience to take notes – especially when properly designed. Here's a handy hint: Instead of reproducing your PowerPoint slides or overheads to full-page size, print them so they occupy 25 to 50 per cent of a page. Then the audience can use the rest of the page to take notes while you speak about each slide or overhead. (Check out the automatic printing format for handouts in PowerPoint.)

Part IV
Delivering Your Presentation or Speech

'So for all you eager investors, our latest financial report will be read to you by our new accountant, Mr Mesmero.'

In this part . . .

It's show time. In this part, we show you how to deliver a speech that wows your audience – that means knowing how to carry yourself, answer questions, and handle any audience no matter how tough or downright weird. You also discover how to convey messages using your voice and body, how to deal with a podium, and how to develop commanding eye contact. These chapters also cover ways to get your audience involved and engaged with your speech. And if you suffer from a touch (or more than a touch) of nervousness, we give you some great ways to overcome it and use it to make your presentation even better.

Chapter 11

Overcoming Nerves

● ●

● ●

*N*ervousness, stage fright, the jitters. The words themselves are enough to make you feel faint. Social scientists may have created other terms to describe nervousness – 'communication anxiety' or 'communication apprehension' – but whatever you want to call it, the symptoms are universally recognised. Your heart pounds. Your hands shake. Your forehead sweats. Your mouth goes dry. Your stomach lurches. And that reaction's just when you get asked to speak in public. You feel really bad when you actually have to give the presentation.

If you do experience a touch of nerves, congratulations; you're in the majority. According to one frequently cited survey, most people consider public speaking more frightening than death. And you're in good company – celebrities alleged to suffer from stage fright include veteran actors such as Laurence Olivier, Peter O'Toole, and Edward Woodward. Although you just have to accept that those feelings of nervousness may always be with you, we discuss some great techniques in this chapter so you can figure out how to control them and use them to your advantage.

Changing Your Perceptions

Teacher to pupil: 'Think positive.' Pupil to teacher: 'I am. I'm positive I'm going to fail.' This old joke highlights an important point – feeling nervous is a purely mental phenomenon. However, if nervousness can be caused mentally, it can be cured mentally. Just consider the way you look at things.

Realising how your audience really feels

Feeling nervous in front of others is a very egocentric affliction. *I'm* scared. *I'm* nervous. *I'm* going to pass out. Me. Me. Me. You may easily lose sight of your audience's interests, but the audience has as much at stake as you. You may suffer from *stage fright* but your audience may be more scared than you. They may suffer from *seat fright* – the fear of wasting time listening to a bad presentation. For you to succeed in giving a great presentation and controlling your fear, you need to know the following four things about your audience:

✔ **The audience wants you to succeed.** By showing up, members of your audience give you a tremendous vote of confidence. They don't want to spend their precious time to come and hear you fail. They want your presentation to be a success. Their success is linked to yours. When your talk is terrific, people in the audience feel good for having turned up.

✔ **You have knowledge that the audience wants.** You were asked to speak for a reason – probably because you have information that the audience desires. You're the expert. You have stories, learning, or data that the audience members are clamouring for. Even on the rare occasion that the audience knows more than you about your topic, you can still provide new information. Only *you* can provide your own unique insights. No one else knows *your* view and interpretation of the material. Think of yourself as sharing valuable knowledge and ideas with your audience.

✔ **The audience doesn't know that you're afraid.** Psychological research shows that the speaker and the audience have very different perceptions about stage fright. Often, an audience can't even detect anxiety in a speaker who claims to be extremely nervous. This situation is like the spot cream advert you see on TV. A typical teenager suffering from acne gets a pimple on his nose. He imagines the pimple is as big as a watermelon and that people are staring at it wherever he goes. Of course, no one even notices it. Nervousness works the same way. Stage fright is a mental pimple that seems a lot worse to you than to your audience.

Visualising success like a pro

The concept of visualisation is simple and straightforward. You just imagine yourself performing a task successfully. Top athletes and sports players use this training technique. They imagine themselves scoring goals, knocking the ball for a six, or getting that hole in one. These people imagine these activities in vivid detail and try to remember past successes and build them into the image.

Popular cures that don't fight fright

Throughout history, human maladies have inspired remedies that claimed fantastic curative powers but actually proved worthless. Snake oil for the common cold. Blood-sucking leeches for fevers. Ear plugs for political speeches. Naturally, a few 'cures' have been offered for stage fright. Here are two famous ones that don't work.

✔ **Imagining the audience naked:** This alleged cure for stage fright is probably as old as human speech itself. We can just see this advice being dispensed by one caveman to another: Caveman 1: 'Don't be nervous; just imagine that the audience is naked.' Caveman 2: 'But they are naked.'

✔ **Taking booze and pills.** Another folk remedy often suggested for nervousness is to have a stiff drink or down a Valium. Doing so is supposed to help you calm down. The problem is: They don't actually make you relaxed, they make you groggy. You feel sleepy and unable to string a coherent sentence together. And then when the effects do wear off, maybe halfway through your presentation, the nerves come back with a vengeance – turning your talk into a far worse nightmare than if you hadn't had that pint or pill.

Apply visualisation techniques to *your* presentation. Imagine yourself giving your talk. Your voice fills the room with wisdom. People in the audience hang on your every word. (If they lean any further forward, they'll fall out of their chairs.) They give you a standing ovation and rush the stage to carry you out on their shoulders.

But don't expect results immediately. Visualisation is like any technique – you get better at it the more you practise. So make sure that you take as many opportunities as you can to visualise success in the run-up to the big day.

Talking yourself into a great presentation

Your audience only has to hear you once. You have to hear yourself all the time, so the messages you send yourself are very important. We're talking about your *internal dialogue* – the little voice that says things to you in your head. When you repeat these messages over and over, you start to believe them. So you've got to be careful what you say. If you keep telling yourself that you'll ruin your presentation at a critical moment, you probably will.

Talking to yourself is the flip side of visualising success – not talking yourself into failure. But the technique involves more than that. Successful visualisation techniques apply to a specific task – like giving a presentation. Your internal dialogue has a much broader focus. It applies to *everything* you do.

So how can you keep the self-chatter positive? Follow these techniques recommended by top psychologists:

> ✔ **Dispute irrational thoughts.** Say that this thought pops into your head: 'If I stand in front of an audience, I'll forget everything I know about the topic.' You need to label it as an irrational thought and challenge it. You can challenge this thought by saying, 'I've never been in a situation in which I've forgotten everything. I've practised this talk six times – so I'm not likely to forget what I'm going to say.'

✔ **Use personal affirmations.** 'I'm the greatest speaker in the world.' 'My subject is fascinating and the audience will love it.' 'I'm an expert.' Yes, they're a little cheesy, but they build confidence. Just as negative thoughts can make you feel worse about yourself, positive thinking can create a relaxed and confident mood. The more you talk yourself into believing your personal affirmations, the less stress you'll encounter with your speech or presentation.

✔ **Imagine the worst-case scenario.** Face your fear directly. Think about the worst possible thing that could happen and realise that it's not that awful. If you make a mistake while you're speaking, you can correct it and continue. If the audience doesn't give you a standing ovation, they may still applaud. Even if the presentation is a total disaster, no one is going to die. A poor presentation isn't the end of the world. Get the situation in perspective.

Transforming Terror to Terrific

A man goes to the doctor for a check-up. He says, 'I look in the mirror and I'm a mess. My skin is sagging. I have blotches all over my face. My hair is falling out. What is it?' The doctor says, 'I don't know, but your eyesight is perfect.'

Unfortunately, a lot of other people have perfect eyesight, too – especially when it involves observing any physical signs that you may be nervous. But thankfully, eliminating or disguising the sweating and shaking isn't that hard.

Discovering stress-busting exercises

Even though stress is technically all in your head, its effects can be quite physical. So if you can't treat your mental state, treat your physical symptoms.

Breathing

Take a deep breath. Hold it. Hold it. Now let it out slowly. Good. Do it again. Breathe deeply and slowly. Really slowly. And keep it up. Don't you feel better already? Breathing slowly is one of the world's oldest techniques for relieving stress. You release carbon dioxide every time you exhale, which decreases the acidity of your blood and increases the flow of oxygen to your brain.

Stretching

Stretching is a great way to relieve muscle tension quickly, and it doesn't take long to do. Stretching for as little as 10 or 15 seconds can be beneficial. Now, you can't just do yoga in the middle of a banquet when you're the after-dinner speaker, but you can excuse yourself and do a few quick stretches in the toilet just a few minutes before you're due to start. Use the following exercises to get you past the finishing line:

- ✓ **Head rolls:** Slowly turn your head from side to side. That's the warm-up. Now move your head clockwise in a circle (look up, right, down, and left). Do this three times and then reverse the direction. You'll feel the tension flowing out of your neck.

- ✓ **Arm lifts:** Stretch your right arm up into the air as far as it will go. Hold it for a few seconds. Bring it back to your side. Now stretch your left arm up as far as it will go. Keep repeating the process. At school, your PE teacher probably made you do this exercise as a form of torture. Now you're going to do it for relief. It helps stretch out your back.

- ✓ **Jaw breakers:** Open your mouth as wide as possible (as if you're going to scream). Then close your mouth. Keep opening and closing your mouth. This exercise helps relieve tension in the jaw. You can also use your fingers to massage the muscle that connects the jaw and the rest of the head.

Moving around

Some speakers like to take a quick walk or jog on the spot to get rid of nervous energy. Are there stairs in the building where you'll speak? A few trips up and down some flights of stairs may be helpful, but don't overdo it. You don't want to be sweaty, tired, and out of breath by the time you go on.

Discovering the real secret: Don't look nervous

A little nervousness is good and a lot of nervousness is bad. So you should control your nervousness and keep it at an acceptable level. You can manage your nervousness by following all the standard techniques described in this chapter.

How nervous you are doesn't really matter – *as long as you appear calm*. All that counts is that the audience thinks you're confident. Try these tips and tricks for disguising some of the common signs of nerves:

- ✔ **Fidgeting:** Fidgeting is an announcement that you're anxious. Touching your face with your index finger or rubbing it under your nose or scratching above your lip or toying with any jewellery are all signs of nervousness. The solution: Keep your hands in front of you in the 'steeple position'. (See Chapter 12 for a description of this position.) If you're using a lectern, place your hands on either side of it or on it as if you're playing the piano.

- ✔ **Pacing:** Pacing is another very visible sign of anxiety. The solution: Move closer to the audience and then stop for a moment. Then move somewhere else and stop.

- ✔ **Sweating:** How you handle the sweating is what counts. If you take a handkerchief, open it up and swipe at the sweat – you look like a nervous wreck. The solution: Never open the handkerchief. Keep it folded in a square. *Dab* at the sweat and then replace the handkerchief in your pocket. If you tend to sweat a lot, wear a t-shirt under your shirt to avoid visible staining.

- ✔ **Hands shaking:** Your hands shaking like a leaf is a pretty good indication of nerves. The solution: Use cards rather than sheets of paper for your notes. Paper, which is larger and weighs less than cards, makes your shakiness more apparent. Also, don't hold props or other items that show that your hands are shaking.

Preventing and Handling Nervousness

Don't be worried about feeling nervous when you're speaking. Just keep the following tips in mind and you'll be ready for anything.

Writing out your intro and conclusion

Nervousness is most intense before you begin speaking. So giving special attention to your introduction is important from a stage-fright perspective. The introduction is the most anxiety-producing part of your presentation or speech. If you write out your introduction and practise it until you have it down pat, you reduce your anxiety.

Similar preparation should be given to the conclusion – often the second most anxiety-producing part of a presentation. (See Chapters 6 and 7 for tips on introductions and conclusions.)

Anticipating problems and preparing solutions

Anticipate any problem that could arise and have a plan ready to deal with it. For example, whenever you stumble over a tongue-twisting name or phrase, you can have an all-purpose recovery line ready: 'Let me try that again – in English.'

What if you forget what point you were going to cover next? You can buy time by asking the audience a survey question that requires a show of hands. Or you can review what you've already covered. Or you can skip ahead to a different point.

Arriving early

Fear of the unknown probably produces more anxiety than any other cause. Until you get to the location where you're presenting, you face a lot of unknowns. Is the room set up correctly? Did they remember to give you an overhead projector?

Plenty of little questions can add up to big sources of stress if you don't have answers for them.

You can get the answers simply by going to the room, so do it early. The earlier you arrive, the more time you have to correct any mistakes and the more time you have to calm down. You may also get a chance to meet members of the audience who arrive early, which can reduce stress by making the audience more familiar to you.

Dividing and conquering

Many speakers who suffer from nervousness claim that what triggers their fear is a large audience. A few people, no problem. A big group, forget it. To cope with a large crowd: Look at one face in the audience at a time – especially faces that appear interested in what you're saying. Keep coming back to these people. (Normally, a basic rule of eye contact is that you shouldn't stare at only a few people and we discuss that in Chapter 12. But overcoming nervousness is the exception. If the only way you can prevent yourself from passing out is to look at only a few people, then do it.)

Not apologising for nervousness

Many speakers feel compelled to apologise for being nervous. Don't apologise for making a mistake. Just let it go. You don't want to draw additional attention to your nervousness.

Using your nervousness

Your nervousness won't go away, so use it to *improve* your delivery. Channelling your nervousness means the next time you speak, you'll have adrenaline coursing through your body – which is no bad thing. Adrenaline is what gives athletes the strength to win that all important race when it counts. And adrenaline's what will give you an extra edge when you give your presentation.

Use your adrenaline rush to give a more animated and enthusiastic performance. Channel your nervous energy into your presentation. Your audience would rather hear and see an 'energised' speaker than one who is falling asleep.

Practising makes perfect – and confident

Familiarity breeds contempt, apparently. But the reverse is true for presentations and public speaking: Familiarity breeds confidence. Practising your presentation can help reduce nerves. Here are a few tips for rehearsing away your fears:

- **Rehearse out loud.** The only way that you can tell how your presentation will sound is to listen to it. *That means that you have to say it out loud.* Practise your talk in an empty office or at home and do it at the volume at which you need to speak. Don't just whisper it out loud. Practise projecting your voice at full volume so you become comfortable with saying the words out loud. Listening to the voice in your head or whispering it meekly don't count – those are not the voices that your audience will hear.

- **Simulate real conditions.** The more closely you can simulate actual speaking conditions in your rehearsals, the more confident you'll be for the actual event. Use the actual notes that you'll use when you present. Use the actual clothes that you'll wear. (At least wear them in your dress rehearsal. That's why dress rehearsals are called dress rehearsals.) Will you be using a handheld microphone for your talk? When you practise at home, use a hairbrush to simulate the microphone so you can get some practice at keeping it close to your mouth at all times.

- **Time it.** Time your presentation. Do it while you're rehearsing in front of an audience. (Audience reactions can affect the length of your talk.) Time your entire presentation. Doing so is the only way to determine whether your talk will fit its assigned time slot. And having that knowledge can relieve a lot of anxiety.

- **Rehearse questions and answers.** If you'll have a question-and-answer period after your presentation, being prepared for it is essential for reducing anxiety. Anticipate questions that you may receive. Rehearse your answers. (For more information about this process, see Chapter 13.)

Chapter 12

Understanding Body Language

. . . .

In This Chapter

▶ Harnessing the power of body language

▶ Establishing commanding eye contact

▶ Dressing for impact

▶ Positioning yourself physically

▶ Using your voice strategically

. . . .

*P*ublic speakers should speak up so they can be heard, stand up so they can be seen, and shut up so they can be enjoyed. That advice may be harsh, but it does highlight a very important aspect of presenting and public speaking: Much of your talk's impact comes from how you look and sound.

Understanding Body Language

Body language refers to the messages you send through facial expression, posture, and gesture. One famous psychological study estimated that nearly 80 per cent of your impact is determined not by *what* you say but *how* you say it. Body language is a language that you already use every day, and most of the meanings are obvious. A smile indicates happiness. A frown signals disapproval. Leaning forward means active engagement in the discussion.

Not as obvious, though, is how *you* employ body language. Watching a videotape of yourself can reveal some amazing insights. Using this method is the quickest way to improve your body language – because the camera doesn't lie. It reveals movements and gestures that you may not know that you're making. Ask someone to videotape you giving a presentation or speech. Then watch the video with the sound off. Common sense tells you most of what you need to correct such as fidgeting with your hands, hunching your shoulders, or repeatedly touching your hair while speaking. Other things to keep in mind are facial expressions, posture, and gestures.

Sending a message with facial expressions

If the eyes are the windows to the soul, then the face is the front of the house. Its appearance says a lot. And how you make your face appear says a lot about your message.

The single most important facial expression is the smile. Simply smiling at an audience can create instant rapport anywhere in the world. A smile is universally understood. Unfortunately, many speakers – particularly business speakers – feel they must wear their 'business face' at all times. They're *serious* businesspeople. They have facts and figures. They have bottom-line responsibilities. If they smile, they might seem . . . human.

You don't need to smile all the time, though. You're not a walking advert for your dentist. In fact, inappropriate smiling can undermine your entire message. But the occasional smile will make your audience warm to you – so don't underestimate its power.

 Use your face to accentuate key points. Act out what you're saying. Are you incredulous about a statistic you've just cited? Raise your eyebrows in disbelief. Are you briefing the audience on a strategy that you disagree with? Frown. Or stick your tongue out at them. (Just kidding. Actually, that action's highly offensive in some cultures. See the 'Going international' section, later in this chapter.)

Punctuating your presentation with posture

Your mother was right. You should always stand up straight – especially when you're giving a speech or presentation. An audience may think a speaker with sloppy posture is lazy, ill, or tired. Likewise, an audience thinks of a speaker with good posture as an upright, confident individual.

The following tips can help you maintain perfect posture:

- ✓ **Stand up straight with your feet slightly apart and your arms ready to gesture.** This is the basic, preferred posture for any presentation or speech.

- ✓ **If you must sit, lean slightly toward the audience.** Leaning forward shows that you're actively engaged with the audience. Leaning back signals retreat.

- ✓ **Lean on the podium only once in a while for effect.** Planting yourself on the podium makes you look weak.

- ✓ **Avoid standing with your hands on your hips.** You'll come across as a bossy PE teacher. Besides, doing so makes you look like you're leading a game of Simon Says. Instead, use your hands to make gestures that enhance your message. For example, if you have three key points, count them out on your fingers.

- ✓ **Avoid swaying back and forth.** Unless you're talking about how to use a metronome or discussing the finer points of seasickness, no one wants to watch you in motion. Swaying back and forth is very distracting. Keep your trunk stationary from the waist up.

- ✓ **Avoid standing with your arms folded across your chest.** You'll look like a thug from a gangster movie. What are you going to do? Beat up the audience? Besides, you should be using your arms to gesture and emphasise your points.

- ✓ **Avoid standing with your arms behind your back.** Doing so limits your ability to gesture. And if you clasp your hands together, it makes you look like you've been hand-cuffed and arrested. Let the audience see your hands as you use them to emphasise points in your presentation.

↳ **Avoid standing in the fig leaf position.** We diagnose this stance when a speaker holds both hands together over his or her crotch – like the fig leaves that Adam and Eve wore. If you're posing for a Renaissance-style painting of blushing modesty this position's fine, but it looks really stupid in any other circumstance. You look as though you want to hide something from your audience. Instead, use your hands to augment your message with gestures.

↳ **Avoid burying your hands in your pockets.** People will wonder what they're doing down there. Putting one hand in your pocket from time to time is fine. But don't leave it there. And make sure never to fiddle with loose change as it really annoys the audience. Having your hands in your pockets also prevents you from using them to gesture.

Giving the right message with gestures

A cynic once suggested that speakers who don't know what to do with their hands should try clamping them over their mouths. That suggestion, though mean-spirited, does highlight a common problem for speakers – what to do with your hands. You can't get around the fact that you have to do *something* with them. And your choice has important consequences for your speech.

Using gestures properly in a speech means breaking one of your mother's basic rules: You *don't* want to keep your hands to yourself. You want to share them with your audience. How do you do that? Just follow these simple guidelines and you'll do fine:

↳ **Create opportunities to use gestures.** If you're worried that gestures won't occur to you naturally, then plan your presentation so that you can include appropriate ones. Include a few items in your talk that beg for gestures. Talk about alternative courses of action, for example 'on the one hand . . . and on the other hand'. Talk about how large or small something is. Talk about how many points you'll make and hold up your fingers. (This technique works best if the number is ten or less.)

✔ **Vary your gestures.** If you make the same gestures repeatedly, you start to look like a robot. And the predictability lowers audience attention levels. Don't let your gestures fall into a pattern. Keep the audience guessing. Doing so keeps them watching. Check out your gesturing habits by videotaping yourself; hit play then fast forward. You can easily see where gestures are repetitive or overdone.

✔ **Put your hands in the steeple position.** Your hands really will take care of themselves as you speak. But if you insist on guidance, just put them together in front of you as if you're applauding. That's the steeple position. Now you don't keep your hands like that. The steeple position's just a rest stop. As you talk, your hands will naturally split apart from the steeple. Sometimes they split widely. Sometimes they split narrowly. The steeple position places your hands in a position where they'll move without your thinking about them. However, too many speakers keep their hands glued together in that position for much too long.

✔ **Make your gestures fit the space.** A common mistake speakers make is transferring gestures used in small, intimate settings to large, formal settings. For example, people at a cocktail party gesture by moving their arms from the elbow to the end of the hand. But if you're speaking to a large audience in a large space, you must adjust your gestures. You must open them up and make them larger. Are you going to emphasise a point? Move your arms from the *shoulders* to the ends of your hands instead of from the elbows.

✔ **Make bold gestures.** Your gestures should communicate confidence and authority. Tentative, half-hearted attempts at gesturing make you look weak and indecisive. Get your hands up. (No, we're not about to rob you.) You'll look more assured if your hands are higher than your elbows. Be bold. Don't use a finger if a fist is more dramatic. Watch politicians speaking in the House of Commons for inspiration.

✔ **Think about your gestures ahead of time, but don't memorise them.** Think about the gestures you'll use. Think about where they may fit into your presentation. But don't plan them your gestures out in specific detail. And don't memorise them. Memorised gestures are obvious to the audience and make you seem robotic.

✔ **Avoid these types of speakers:**

- **The banker:** They keep rattling coins in their pockets. They sound like a change machine. The sound is very distracting.

- **The optician:** They constantly adjust their glasses. They're on. They're off. They're slipping down their noses. Do everyone a favour and avoid touching your glasses – or get some contact lenses.

- **The tailor:** They fiddle with their clothing. The tie is a big object of affection for male speakers in this category. They twist it. And pinch it. And rub it. No one listens to the talk. We're all waiting to see if the speaker will choke himself.

- **The jeweller:** They fiddle with their jewellery. Necklaces are a big attraction for female speakers in this category. And you'll find ring twisters of both genders.

- **The lonely lover:** They hug themselves. This position looks really weird. They stand up in front of the audience and put their arms round themselves while they speak. They lose a lot of credibility.

- **The beggar:** They clasp their hands together and thrust them toward the audience as if they're begging for something. They probably are – a miracle.

- **The hygienist:** They keep rubbing their hands together like they're washing them. Doing so looks weird for a few reasons. There's no soap. No water. No sink. And a load of people called an audience is watching.

- **The toy maker:** They love to play with their little toys – pens, markers, pointers – whatever happens to be around. They turn them in their hands. They squeeze them. And they distract the audience.

- **The hair stylist:** They keep flicking, pulling, or rearranging their hair. Yes, the audience knows you've just got a nervous habit, but they still wonder when you last washed your hair.

Going international

As if standing up and giving a presentation or speech isn't already tough enough, it takes on a whole new level of difficulty when you address audiences from around the world. Cultural differences come into play. And navigating the proprieties of appropriate body language is as simple as walking through a minefield without a map.

To get through your presentation without causing offence, start by following one basic rule: Remember that body language isn't universal. So how do you know if your body language will be offensive?

Here are some general guidelines for using body language successfully when you speak around the globe:

- ✓ **Speaking to a northern European audience:** Northern European audiences prefer a formal style, and that preference is reflected in a low-key use of body language. North Europeans such as Germans and Scandinavians don't tend to like high-energy styles with emphatic gestures and lots of walking back and forth across the stage. They consider that type of delivery shallow and it lowers the speaker's credibility.

- ✓ **Speaking to a southern European audience:** Southern Europeans including the Spanish and Italians are a bit more relaxed than our northern European counterparts and much prefer a bit more energy and emphasis. So allow yourself some of the more expansive gestures and feel free to walk around the stage area a bit if you like.

- ✓ **Speaking to a North American audience:** North American audiences appreciate an animated style of delivery. So allow yourself to make bigger gestures and to be more passionate. And these audiences iare quite happy for presenters to stride all over the stage when speaking, too.

- ✓ **Speaking to an Asian audience:** Asian audiences are perhaps just a little bit more formal than the Brits, but generally the same rules apply. However, Asian audiences will be attentive and respectful even if the speaker isn't any good.

✔ **Speaking to a South American audience:** South American audiences like a speaker who is decisive. That means gestures and movement can be expansive and emphatic.

These general guidelines can help you plan a speech to international audiences, but the only way to be sure that specific gestures won't be offensive is to talk with people from that culture before you turn up. So make sure you ask your contact questions about what may be appropriate before you set off.

Making Eye Contact Count

At some point in many old tear-jerker romantic films, the heroine tells the hero (or vice versa) that she doesn't love him anymore. (Usually the villain has forced this situation upon them.) The violins rise up strongly on the soundtrack. The camera pans in for a close-up. Shock and disbelief register across the hero's face. And inevitably he utters this immortal line: 'Look me in the eye and say that.' The hero means that her words aren't true until she says them while making eye contact.

'If looks could kill.' We've all been glad they can't when we've been on the receiving end of this statement, but when you give a presentation or speech, looks *can* kill. Depending on what you do or don't look at, looks can kill your entire presentation. Use the following rules to prevent yourself from committing a criminal offence:

✔ **Look at individuals.** As you gaze around the room, make eye contact with as many individuals as possible. A common myth is to pick out a friendly face and look at it. That quickly seems weird. This poor person wonders why you're staring at him or her, and so does the rest of the audience. Look at a variety of individuals. Remember, you want to be a search light, not a laser beam.

✔ **Establish eye contact at the end of a thought.** Eye contact is most effective at this point. People will nod their heads under the pressure of your gaze, and their doing so is a big plus for you. Because of the structure of English sentences, the important information is usually in the second half of the sentence; so, making eye contact at the end of a thought emphasises the important part. By making eye contact in this way, you force people to nod when you make a point. That nodding doesn't automatically mean that they agree with you, but it subconsciously forces the audience in that direction.

- ✔ **Look at the audience, not everywhere else.** If you look out the window, so will your audience. This fact is also true for looking at the ceiling, the walls, or the floor. The audience plays follow the leader, and you're the leader. Look at them so they'll look at you.

- ✔ **Look at more than one spot.** Make sure that you establish eye contact with all parts of your audience. Cover the entire room. If you look straight ahead and never look toward the sides or if you look only at the people toward the front, you risk losing a major portion of your audience because everyone towards the side and in the back feels left out. No, you don't want your head to look like a machine gun pivoting back and forth as it sprays eye contact at the crowd. But you do want to keep your gaze rotating from one part of the audience to another.

- ✔ **Spend more time looking at the audience than your notes.** Some speakers get so hung up looking at their notes that they don't look at thepeople in front of them. Big mistake. The notes aren't going to applaud when you're done. And neither will the audience if you haven't looked at them. Ideally, you should rehearse your talk enough so that you don't need to refer to your notes much at all. But if you must read from them, first make sure your notes are easy to read – large print, legible, only a few key words per card. Second, watch how TV news presenters read from their notes. They look down. They read the notes. They look up. They look into the camera. They tell you one thought. Then they repeat the process. Head up. Head down. Head up. Head down. (Just don't do it too fast or you'll look like a nodding dog on a car dashboard.)

- ✔ **Look at the noses of the audience if you're nervous, not over their heads.** A big myth of giving presentations is that gazing over the heads of your audience is okay. But people can tell if you're speaking to the clock on the back wall. And the smaller the audience, the more obvious this technique becomes. If you're too nervous to look in your audience's eyes, just look at the tips of their noses – it works.

Dressing to Impress

A single article of clothing can change your entire image and have a large effect on how an audience receives your message. Although it may be shallow, people make all kinds of judgements based on clothes. Doing so's human nature. Many studies of clothes shops have shown that well-dressed customers receive better service than poorly dressed ones. And the same goes for giving presentations. Your clothing is part of your message, and it should augment what you say, not detract from it.

Getting the right image across

Use the following handy tips to help you dress appropriately for any speaking engagement:

- ✔ **Dress conservatively (especially in Europe, Asia, and South America).** You want your audience to focus on you – not on what you're wearing. Even more important, informal attire may lower your credibility if your audience is all suited and booted.

- ✔ **Shine your shoes.** The audience will see them – especially if you're standing on a stage.

- ✔ **Wear comfortable clothes.** That doesn't mean old clothes or informal clothes. It means that maybe the time to break in that new pair of shoes isn't the day you're giving your presentation.

- ✔ **Keep the pencils, pens, and markers from peeking out of your shirt or jacket pockets.** It makes you look like a computer geek.

- ✔ **Wear jewellery that won't distract the audience.** Distraction is defined as when your jewellery is louder than you are (both to the eye and ear).

- ✔ **Leave your briefcase or handbag somewhere other than the podium.** Items on stage are a distraction. Ask someone to guard it for you.

> ✔ **Keep bulky stuff out of your pockets.** Remember Mae
> West's famous line, 'Is that a pistol in your pocket or are
> you just happy to see me?' You don't want the audience
> wondering what's in your pockets, whether you're a man
> or a woman; you want them wondering what you're going
> to say next.

Dressing for informal meetings

Say that you're presenting at an event where the audience will
be dressed casually – golf clothes, shorts, t-shirts, and maybe
even swimming costumes. Is it okay for you to dress casually?
Great minds diverge, but if you're speaking at a business event,
we'd warn you to at least dress up slightly more than your
audience. You may wish to dress down a bit – you don't want
to be wearing a tie if everyone in the audience is in swimwear.
So if the audience are all in shorts, maybe at least wear long
trousers and a polo shirt or a smart-casual skirt and top.

You ought to dress a little more formally because the audience takes your message more seriously if you look more serious. Also, speakers who dress entirely casually may fall into
the trap of speaking too casually. The exception to dressing
smarter than your audience is when you're also a member of
the audience you're addressing. Say that a group of managers
is dressed in golf clothes because golf is scheduled right after
the meeting. You're one of the managers in the meeting, so
you'll be playing golf just like everyone else, and you're scheduled to make a presentation during the meeting. In that situation, you probably want to be wearing golf clothes. *Not*
wearing them would seem odd and detract from your talk.

Whatever the situation, the criterion is always identical. Wear
the attire that will most enhance your message.

Mastering Physical Positioning and Movement

Although you may have your intro down pat and think you're
totally prepared to give your presentation, you may have
forgotten that getting to and from the podium, as well as

standing and moving when you're there have important consequences for your talk. So check out the tips we provide in the sections below to make sure your presentation gets started on the right foot.

Managing entrances and exits

Imagine your name being announced. You get up to move towards the podium and stumble. Your notes go flying and you knock a glass of water on to the stage. Not a good entrance. Not how you want your entrances, or exits, to be remembered.

Getting onstage with class

The beginning of a presentation or speech is its most critical part. Everyone knows that. But when does it begin? Does your presentation kick off when you start speaking? When you walk to the podium? When you enter the room?

We believe your presentation starts almost from the moment you leave home. The next few paragraphs walk you through how you should begin your presentation, starting from home.

After you leave your home, you never know when a member of your audience may see you. And if you're observed engaging in some questionable activity, your image may suffer. When you ascend the stage to speak, you want to project an aura of confidence and command. You want to be all-powerful. You don't want any audience members to recall that an hour ago they saw you eating a greasy burger on the steps of the conference centre or picking your teeth in the car park.

Get to the room early and make sure that the podium, microphone, and any audiovisual equipment are arranged properly. Pay particular attention to microphone cords and power cords. You don't want to open your talk by tripping and falling. If you're speaking on a stage, check where the steps up to it are located. Plan your route to the podium and practise it before your speech if possible.

While you're waiting to speak, listen attentively to any speakers preceding you. When you're introduced, rise confidently and walk assuredly to the podium. Shaking hands with the person who introduced you is optional. (Unless the person extends his or her hand!)

When you arrive at the podium, place your notes where you want them. Open them. Look out at the audience. Pause. Then give a fantastic presentation.

Getting offstage in style

Saying the last words of your speech is only the beginning of the end. You still have a lot to do. And that doesn't mean hurriedly gathering up your notes and getting out of there. First and foremost, you must bask in the thundering ovation that your audience will no doubt deliver. (If, for some unfathomable reason, they're not immediately forthcoming with applause, then you can give them a hint. If you're feeling brave, anyway. When a deafening roar of approval doesn't greet your closing, you could make a short bowing motion with your head and shoulders. The audience usually get the message.)

After you've accepted your ovation (and answered any questions), you must disconnect yourself from the microphone (if you were using a clip-on device). Many speakers forget this step, and it can be quite embarrassing. Even if you don't wear the mike into the toilet, everyone still hears you breathing, and you lose credibility.

After the microphone is detached, gather your speaking materials and depart from the podium in a confident manner. Stride purposefully back to your seat. Smile and acknowledge audience acclaim along the way. If you're followed by another speaker, become a model audience member. Wait expectantly for the speaker with your full attention directed at the podium.

Act this way even if you've just given the world's worst presentation. Amazingly, people will give you the reaction you ask for. If *you* act like the presentation was a success (even if it wasn't), a better than average chance exists that the audience will play along. Doing so makes *everybody* feel better.

You're never really finished until you've left the site of your presentation, you no longer have contact with any audience members (such as in a hotel bar after your talk), and you're home in bed.

Moving around

People have short attention spans today. And movement helps maintain audience attention. Of course, speakers who move endlessly and erratically will distract from their message. Follow these tips to have all the right moves:

- ✔ **Use up and down movements.** Find a reason to bend over close to the floor or reach up into the air. These movements – used very occasionally – can make you look more interesting to the audience.

- ✔ **Move purposefully.** Make every movement count. Whether you're gesturing, changing position, or walking from one location to another, the movement must support your message. Pacing is an example of *non*-purposeful movement that you should avoid.

- ✔ **Be aware of audience depth perception.** If you're speaking from a stage in a large room, moving left or right has much more impact than moving forward or back. (This phenomenon is created by depth perception. Don't ask us to explain it.) Remembering this effect is important because it goes against instinct. You may assume that moving toward or away from the audience has the bigger effect. It doesn't. A step forward or back doesn't have half the impact of a step left or right. Keep that in mind when you want to emphasise a point.

- ✔ **Move in an irregular pattern.** A major value of movement is that it helps maintain audience attention. But moving in a regular pattern has an opposite effect. The predictability of any regular pattern lulls the audience into a semi-hypnotic state (also known as sleep). You want to keep moving. Just make sure no one else knows where you're going.

- ✔ **Avoid making nervous movements.** Speakers who constantly pull at their hair, shift from foot to foot, play with their notes, scratch themselves, and adjust their clothes are very distracting. So avoid those types of nervous movements. Don't be a perpetual motion machine. You'll end up looking very nervous or as though you need the toilet. Either way, the audience won't focus on what you're saying.

Getting into the power position

For those of you dragging out a yoga mat now, when we say *power position* we're talking about the power position when you're speaking from a stage. To find this spot, divide the stage into a three by three, nine-square grid: back left, back centre, back right, left centre, centre centre, right centre, front right, front centre, front left. The power position is front centre.

But don't just stand in this position. Move into different squares as you speak. If you want a mechanical formula, find cues in your talk that suggest moves. 'I was in a cattle shop looking at bulls. And over on the right I saw (move to a square on the right) a beautiful set of china teacups. I took one to the proprietor (move into another square) and I said, "Is this the famous china in a bull shop?"' (Now you'd better move to a rear square because with puns like that, the audience may start throwing things.)

This process of moving from square to square is called making an active stage picture. Doing so ensures that you don't just stand in one place, and it makes you more interesting for the audience to watch. Just remember to return frequently to the power square.

Working from a podium

Many people believe that podiums act as a barrier between the speaker and the audience – that the speaker is 'hiding' behind the podium. So, many public speaking teachers, communication coaches, and other professional presenter types give this advice: Don't use a podium. Nowadays, presentations are as much about entertainment as information. And if you do use a podium, get out from behind it as often as possible.

However, if you feel nervous without a podium and you want to use one, then go ahead.

Two reasons exist why you may want to use a podium, and the first is common sense:

1. **If you're comfortable behind a podium and nervous in front of it, then stay behind it.** You'll give a better presentation. Getting out from behind the podium to 'eliminate a barrier with your audience' is pointless if doing so creates a bigger barrier – crippling nervousness (see Chapter 11 for more on coping with nerves).

2. **Eye contact is more important than being able to see your body.** An audience's first connection with you is always with your facial expression and eye contact. So long as you're making good eye contact and using a range of appropriate facial expressions to animate your face, it doesn't matter if the audience can't see your body. However, stepping away from the podium occasionally (if you feel confident enough to do so) can be a good change for your audience.

Using the podium effectively

Just like anything else you do while giving your presentation, using a podium does have guidelines; check them out below:

✔ **Use the podium as a strategic tool.** The podium doesn't just have to be a place where you dump your notes and give your speech or presentation. The podium can play a much more active role in your talk. Timing is a perfect example. Say you ask your audience a rhetorical question and want them to ponder on the answer. Try turning your back on them and walking away for a few seconds. By the time you return to the podium, your audience should have had a few seconds to think about your question.

✔ **Look at your notes while you're moving behind the podium.** Want to disguise your reliance on notes? Look at your notes whenever you move. When you make a gesture, shift position, or turn your head, take a quick peek at your notes. Like a magician's hand, the audience will focus on your movement rather than what you're actually doing – reading.

✔ **Use a podium to 'hide' when appropriate.** Even if you don't like to stay behind a podium, sometimes you may need to draw audience attention to something other than yourself. Are you using PowerPoint slides, overheads, or a volunteer from the audience? Standing behind a podium makes perfect sense for these situations, especially if the podium is placed off to the side.

✓ **Avoid pressing or gripping the podium.** Using a podium is okay – but not as a crutch. Standing rigidly behind your podium is a sign that you're not as confident as the audience would like you to be.

Gripping the podium for dear life is another common mistake – like you'll float away if you let go. Again, your behaviour's disconcerting for the audience, because clinging to the podium is an obvious indication of extreme nervousness. Instead of concentrating on what the speaker is saying, the audience is mentally placing bets on when he or she will pass out.

Paralanguage: What Your Voice Says about You

People don't just judge you by what you say – they also judge you by how you say it. Do you say the words loudly? Rapidly? Monotonously? Do you have an accent? Do you mispronounce words? All of these factors – *how* you say things, not *what* you say – are known as *paralanguage*.

Here are some tricks and tips for using your voice.

✓ **Warm up your voice.** You're about to speak. You're opening line is a gem. People will be quoting it for years. You're introduced. You get to the podium. You open your mouth to deliver your *bon mots* and . . . your voice cracks. So much for the brilliant opening. That's why you need to warm up your voice. Find an empty room or pop into the toilet before you speak and do some vocal exercises. Hum. Talk to yourself. Get your voice going. (But make sure that no one is in there with you. You *don't* want anyone in the audience to remember you as the person talking to themself in the loo.) *Singing For Dummies* by Pamelia S. Phillips (Wiley) has several excellent exercises for warming up your voice that work just as well for speaking as they do for singing.

✓ **Pronounce your words clearly.** You know that speaking with your mouth full isn't polite. Well, sounding like you're speaking with your mouth full isn't polite either – especially if you have an audience. It can be hard enough for one person to understand another even when they each know exactly what was said. Don't make communication even more difficult. Pronounce your words clearly.

✔ **Get rid of filler sounds and phrases.** Filler sounds and phrases take up space for no reason, sound stupid, and distract the audience from your message. Banish these words and phrases from your vocabulary: Like, you know, um, okay, ugh, ah, actually, interestingly enough.

✔ **Use vocal variety.** Monotony refers to more than just tone of voice. Yes, a monotonous voice may be the result of speaking in one tone. But it may also result from speaking at one rate of speed, in one volume, or in one pitch. If you're monotonous in any of those ways, you have a problem. If you're monotonous in all of those ways, the audience will fall asleep. The cure is vocal variety. Speed up to express excitement. Slow down if you need your audience to take heed of a warning message.

✔ **Use your voice for emphasis.** You can completely alter the meaning of a sentence simply by changing the words you emphasise. Say the following line aloud and emphasise the word in italics. 'Are you talking to *me*?' 'Are *you* talking to me?' 'Are you *talking* to me?' Alright, enough with the Robert DeNiro impressions. You get the idea. Use vocal emphasis to reinforce the meanings you want to communicate.

✔ **Slow down after mistakes.** No one is perfect. Everyone makes mistakes. Inevitably, you'ill mispronounce a word or stumble through a tongue-twisting phrase. The natural instinct is to speed up when you make a mistake. Don't. Doing so highlights your error and increases your chances for making additional errors. So slow down.

✔ **Use volume as a tool.** Volume is a powerful tool that you can easily manipulate. Changing your pitch or tone may be difficult, but anyone can speak more loudly or softly. Try dropping your voice to a conspiratorial whisper as if you're conveying a secret. Or try raising your voice when you are talking about how exciting a new opportunity could be. Doing so can have an amazing effect on an audience.

Many speakers think you should never speak softly. Wrong. Speaking softly can be incredibly effective. We've seen speakers whisper and draw in an entire audience. People lean forward in their seats. How can they hear? If you're speaking into a microphone, speaking softly doesn't matter. The whole point of using the microphone is that it allows you to speak in a full range of volumes.

Speaking at a high volume can also be used dramatically. If you're telling a tale of some struggle or argument, it may be appropriate to yell some of the dialogue. Just make sure you don't overdo it. You want to entertain your audience, not shock them into a stunned silence.

Any time you shift your volume, people will pay attention. Volume's an easy way to vary your speech pattern. So use it.

✓ **Use pauses.** A common mistake among inexperienced (and nervous) speakers is to speak without pausing. They just rush through their talks, one thought merging into another. The audience *listens* to a lot of words but don't *hear* a thing. They become clogged with information.

The pause is a vital part of the communication process. It leaves time for the meaning of what's been said to sink in. And a pause clears the way for the importance of what comes next. Also, pausing before a change of subject, major point, or interesting fact creates an impression of confidence. Pausing also highlights the point. Don't be afraid to use pauses.

Chapter 13

Handling Questions

· ·

In This Chapter

▶ Checking out some basic guidelines

▶ Designing a perfect answer

▶ Answering questions with six techniques

▶ Responding to common types of questions

▶ Dealing with special situations

▶ Discovering how to handle hostile questions

· ·

A professor travelled from university to university speaking about quantum physics. One day his chauffeur said, 'Professor, I've heard your lecture so many times I could give it myself.' The professor said, 'Fine. Give it tonight.' When they got to the university, the chauffeur was introduced as the professor. The chauffeur delivered the lecture, and nobody knew the difference. Afterward, someone in the audience asked a long question about Boolean algebra and quantum mechanics. The chauffeur didn't miss a beat. He said, 'I can't believe you asked that question. It's so simple, I'm going to let my chauffeur answer it.'

Unfortunately, most people don't have a chauffeur who can answer tough questions. So you have to drive yourself through the maze known as the question-and-answer session. Many speakers let their guard down during this session. Doing so's a big mistake. Even if you gave a great presentation, a poor performance during the question and answer (Q&A) session can totally change the audience's perceptions of you and your topic. Equally, if your presentation was mediocre, a strong performance during the Q&A can leave the audience with a very positive impression. So, read the rest of this chapter to make sure you give a great performance during the Q&A (but read the rest of this book to make sure the rest of your presentation is a hit, too!)

Discovering the Basics

To give a sparkling performance during a question and answer session, stack the odds in your favour by following a few basic rules.

Anticipate questions

The secret to giving brilliant answers is knowing the questions in advance. In some circles, this ability is called clairvoyance. (In a school exam, it's called cheating.) In our system, knowing the questions is called anticipation. You anticipate what you'll be asked.

Just use your common sense to anticipate questions. Think about your presentation and your audience. Then generate a list of every possible question that the audience may ask. Don't pull any punches. Think of the toughest questions that may come up. Then ask your colleagues or friends to think of the toughest questions they can devise, too.

After you've compiled a comprehensive list of questions, prepare an answer for each one. Practise saying your answers out loud until you feel comfortable with them. With a little on-the-spot tweaking, they may also help you answer questions that you didn't anticipate.

Answer questions at the end

Taking questions *after* you've made your presentation is generally better than while you're giving it. If you take questions during your talk, it distracts both you and the audience, it makes your presentation harder to follow, and it can ruin your rhythm. (Someone asking a question just as you're building to the climax of your most dramatic story is always thrilling.) Unless you're a very confident presenter, tell the audience at the beginning that you'll take questions at the end.

Don't let a few people dominate

Every so often, you get an audience from which one or two people ask questions – endlessly. The moment you finish answering their first questions, they're asking others. Whatever their motivation, your job is not to play 20 questions with them. You want to have a conversation with the *entire* audience, not just one or two members of it.

Try to take questions from as many different audience members as time permits. Don't let a couple of people ask all the questions, unless they're the only ones with questions. Doing so just frustrates everyone else whose hand is raised, wanting to ask you something. Eventually such audience members just give up.

Be fair. Don't favour one section of the room over another. The best approach is to try to call on people in the order in which they raised their hands. Don't give in to bullies who don't wait their turn and instead shout out questions. Shouting out is the oral equivalent of jumping a queue, and is definitely not fair to the people who have been patiently waiting for you to call on them.

Establish the ground rules early. When you open the session up for questions, tell the audience that everyone will initially be limited to a single question. Then if time permits, you'll take a second round of questions.

Encourage questioners to ask questions, not to give speeches

You just asked for questions. Despite the fact that you're standing at a podium and you've just given a lengthy presentation, someone in the audience is bound to want to give a presentation-length speech, too. One of these people exists in every crowd, and your job is to make sure they don't launch into a speech.

You're the speaker. You opened up the session for questions – not speeches. When one of these people starts giving a speech, you must cut it off. How do you do it? Try gently interrupting the person and suggest a question: 'So what you're really asking is. . .' (If the reply is, 'No, that's not what I'm asking,' then immediately say, 'Could you state your question, please?')

Listen to the question

If you want to be successful in a question and answer session, then you need to listen. We mean *really* listen: Go below the surface of the words used by the questioner; read between the lines; watch the body language; and listen to the tone of voice. Doing so enables you to identify what the questioner is really asking. Yes, intensely listening is exhausting (and you still have to look fresh and dapper – see Chapter 12 for more on appearance), but your answers will be infinitely better if you really listen to every question.

Repeat the question

Not repeating the question you've been asked is an enormous mistake. Nothing is more frustrating than giving a brilliant answer to a question that wasn't asked.

Three major reasons exist why you should *always* repeat the question:

- ✔ You make sure that everyone in the audience heard the question.

- ✔ You make sure that *you* heard the question correctly.

- ✔ You buy yourself some time to think about your answer. (If you want even more time, rephrase the question slightly and say, 'Is that the essence of what you're asking?')

If a question is lengthy or confusing, don't repeat it word for word. Rephrase it so that you make it concise and understandable.

Don't guess

If you don't know the answer to a question, never guess. *Never.* Doing so's a one-way ticket to zero credibility. Once in a while you may get lucky, beat the odds, and bluff the audience. But most of the time, someone will call your bluff. Then you have a big problem. First, you'll be exposed as not knowing the answer you claim to know. More important, the audience wonders if you bluffed about anything else.

If you don't know the answer to a question, admit it. Then take one, some, or all of the following actions:

- ✔ Ask if anyone in the audience can answer the question.
- ✔ Suggest a resource where the questioner can find the answer.
- ✔ Offer to discover the answer yourself and get it to the questioner.

Remember, nobody knows everything!

End the Q&A strongly

The Q&A session is your last chance to influence audience opinion – of your topic, your ideas, and you. So you want a strong ending. Keep these two things in mind:

- ✔ **End the session on a high note.** Don't wait for audience questions to die off and say, 'Well, I guess that's it.' You'll look weak and not in control.
- ✔ **Make sure the last question you get is one that you can answer.** Don't say, 'We only have time for one more question.' It may be a question you can't answer or handle well. Again, answering poorly will make you look weak.

After you've answered a reasonable number of questions, start looking for an opportunity to end the session. Wait till you get a question that you answer brilliantly. Then announce that time has run out. Of course, you'll be happy to stick around and speak with anyone who still has a question.

What if you don't get any questions that you can answer brilliantly? Don't worry. Just make the last question one that you ask yourself. 'Thank you. We've run out of time. Well, actually you're probably still wondering about [fill in your question].' Then give your brilliant answer.

One more word (actually four) about ending the Q&A session: End it on time. Some audience members come solely for your presentation and may need to leave. They don't care about the Q&A. (Or they don't care about the questions being asked.) So stick to the schedule. You can make yourself available afterward for anyone who wants to keep the discussion going.

Coming Up with a Perfect Answer

Apparently experts are people who know all the right answers – if they're asked the right questions. Unfortunately, your audience may not always ask the right questions. This section presents some ways to make sure your answers will be expert, no matter what you're asked.

Treating the questioner properly

Questioners may be rude, obnoxious, opinionated, egomaniacal, inane, obtuse, antagonistic, befuddled, illiterate, or incomprehensible. You still have to treat them nicely. Why? Because they're members of the audience, and the audience identifies with them – at least initially. Use these suggestions for dealing with someone who asks you a question:

- ✔ **Assist a nervous questioner.** Some audience members who ask questions may suffer from a touch of nervousness themselves. These people want to ask their question so much that they try to ignore their pounding hearts, sweaty palms, and stomach cramps. As they ask their questions, they try to forget that all eyes in the room are on them, but ignoring this situation is often difficult. So anxious audience members having trouble getting out their questions isn't unusual. They'll stammer and stutter, they'll lose their train of thought, and they'll make the rest of the audience extremely uncomfortable. Help these people out. Finish asking their questions for them if you can. Otherwise, offer some gentle encouragement. By breaking in and speaking yourself, you give nervous questioners time to collect themselves. They'll be grateful. And so will everyone else.

✓ **Wait for the questioner to finish.** Unless the questioners are rambling or they're nervous and need help, let them finish asking their questions. Too many speakers jump in before the question is fully stated. They *think* they know what the question is, and they start giving an answer. They look very foolish when the questioner interrupts saying, 'That's not what I was asking.' Only interrupt the questioner if they're using the opportunity to give a little speech of their own.

✓ **Recognise the questioner by name.** If you know the name of the person asking the question, use it. Doing so has a powerful effect on the audience. It makes you seem much more knowledgeable and in control. And the people whose names you say always appreciate the recognition.

✓ **Compliment the questioner, if appropriate.** If the question is particularly interesting or intelligent, saying so is okay. But be specific and say why. Some communication gurus advise never to say, 'Good question' because doing so implies that the other questions weren't. To avoid offending anyone, say, 'That's an especially interesting question because. . .' This statement implies that the other questions were also interesting – a compliment. Phrasing your response that way also eliminates all the value judgements attached to the word 'good'.

✓ **Treat the questioner with dignity.** Yes, the question may be inane or even stupid. But you don't want to be the one to point it out. No matter how idiotic the query, treat the questioner with dignity. If you imply that the question was stupid, you make yourself look bad, generate sympathy for the questioner, and discourage anyone else from asking questions.

✓ **Look fascinated as they ask their questions.** For a questioner to rise out of the anonymity of the audience to ask a question can take a lot of guts, so don't discourage questioners by looking bored or condescending while they're speaking. Even if you think the question is silly, look fascinated. Give each questioner your full attention. Make eye contact. Lean forward. Nod while they are speaking to show that you're listening. Show that your most important priority is listening to the question. Nothing is more insulting or dispiriting than a speaker who looks around the audience for the next question while the current question is being asked. And not only the questioner is offended. The whole audience picks up on the negative nonverbal message.

✔ **Stay calm and in control.** No matter how offensive the question or questioner, don't attack them. Use diplomacy and finesse to dispose of such annoyances. If the questioner is a major annoyance, the audience will recognise it. Don't become an annoyance yourself by getting defensive. The questioner wants to provoke you. Don't take the bait. (See Chapter 14 for more on hecklers.)

Designing your answer

You never know exactly how to answer until you receive the question, but knowing that isn't really helpful if you're trying to prepare in advance. The following general guidelines can help you formulate your answers:

✔ **Keep it brief.** Your answer should be a simple, succinct response to the question asked. Too many speakers use their answer as an excuse to give a second presentation. Give everyone a break. If the audience wanted an encore, it would have asked for one. And remember, many members of the audience may not even be interested in the question you're answering. They may be waiting to hear the next question – or ask one.

✔ **Refer back to your presentation.** Tying your answers back to your talk reinforces the points you made earlier. This tactic also makes you seem omniscient. (You somehow foresaw these questions and planted the seeds of their answers in your presentation.)

✔ **Define the terms under discussion.** Say someone asks if you think the middle class deserves a tax cut. You say, 'Yes.' The questioner immediately disagrees by arguing that giving a tax break to the middle class is unfair. After a ten-minute debate, everyone realises that no real disagreement exists. You don't think any family making more than £100,000 deserves a tax break, and neither does the questioner, but you define such families as 'rich'. The questioner defines them as 'middle class'. Make sure that everyone is on the same wavelength. Define the terms of what you're talking about up front.

✔ **Refer to your experience.** Referring to your personal and professional experience in your answer isn't bragging. That experience is one of the reasons you've been invited to present and part of what makes you an expert. The audience *wants* to hear about your experience. Just don't do it for every single question.

✔ **Point out misconceptions stated by the questioner and firmly state your position.** Never let a questioner define your position. An alarm should go off when you hear a questioner say something like, 'Well, based on your talk, it's obvious that you think. . .' Typically, what the questioner says you think, *isn't* what you think at all. Don't let anyone put words in your mouth. If this situation occurs, address the problem immediately – as soon as the questioner finishes asking the question.

✔ **Dispute the questioner's facts or stats if you disagree.** Don't get locked into the questioner's facts or premises. If the questioner makes assumptions with which you disagree, politely say so. If you dispute the questioner's statistics, say so. Don't build a nice answer on a faulty question. Start by dismantling the question.

✔ **Be honest.** Don't make promises you won't keep. Don't say that anyone can call you at your office to ask questions if you know you won't take their calls. Don't say you'll find out the answer to a question if you know you won't. Don't offer to send information to someone if you know you'll never get around to it.

✔ **You can politely decline to answer a question.** But don't evade questions by acting like you're answering them. You're not obligated to answer every question. (You're *really not* under interrogation although a Q&A may sometimes seem that way.) But if you evade questions, you lose credibility. Doing so looks like you're ducking the issues. If you don't want to answer a question, say so firmly and politely. State the reasons why and move on to the next question.

✔ **Raise all of your points in your presentation, rather than hoping to be asked a particular question.** Leaving important points out of your presentation because you want to save them for the Q&A session is dangerous. If no one asks the right questions, you may never get a chance to make those points.

Delivering your answer

Having the perfect answer doesn't mean much if you can't deliver it effectively. But don't worry. The following simple rules ensure that your response will be – well, perfect.

✔ **Have the appropriate attitude.** Match your demeanour to the substance of the question and your answer. If someone is confused, be understanding. If someone is blatantly offensive, be forceful and disapproving (without counterattacking). If someone is seeking information, be professorial. Never lose control of yourself. Never be discourteous.

✔ **Look at the entire audience.** Don't limit eye contact to the questioner. Start off by looking at the questioner, but as you give your answer, direct your eye contact to the entire audience. You're speaking to everyone – not just the questioner.

✔ **Avoid being smug.** This attitude doesn't win any accolades from the audience, and it just creates a barrier. Being smug can also backfire in a big way: The audience starts rooting for you to screw up. The first time you fumble an answer – even if you're just mis-stating an insignificant detail – smugness comes back to haunt you.

Using Question-Handling Techniques

How do you become an expert in deftly fielding questions? Practice. Practise what? The following six basic techniques can help you build your question-handling skills.

Reversing the question

Someone in your audience may ask you a question for the express purpose of putting you on the spot. No sweat. Just reverse it. For example, the questioner makes a big show of appearing bored and asks, 'What time are we going to take a break?' Don't get defensive. Just respond, 'What time would you like to take a break?' This process is mental judo. You use the weight of the questioner's own question against them.

Redirecting the question

Someone asks a question. You don't have the faintest idea how to answer it. What can you do? Get the audience involved. Redirect the question to the entire group. Say, 'That's an interesting question. Does anyone have any thoughts on the subject?' Or, 'Does anyone have any experience with that situation?' The audience is a great resource; take advantage of it.

Rephrasing the question

'Last week's news that your chief executive will stand trial for bribing a minister has finally revealed how your parasitic company got government approval for a drug that's already killed 200 people. Will you now issue a recall to remove it from the market?' Hmmm. Are you really supposed to repeat this question for the audience? Of course, the questioner is pretending to ask a question but is really making an attack. So don't repeat back the question. In fact, you never want to repeat a question that presents a problem – doing so is embarrassing, difficult, hard to follow, whatever. So, although you shouldn't repeat the question word for word, you should rephrase it to your advantage. 'The question is about how we will convert our concern for public safety into action. Here are the steps we are taking to protect the public. . .'

Keep in mind that a question can be a problem just because the questioner has worded it in an obtuse manner. 'In your opinion, will the actions of the Bank of England to control inflation through monetary policy, combined with global financial trends – particularly the devaluation of the Euro –

result in economic forces that validate or prove wrong the City bulls in the short term?' Huh? Rephrase the question so that the audience can understand it (assuming *you* can understand it). Such a response may be, 'If I understand correctly, the question is whether the stock market will go up or down in the next few months.'

Exposing a hidden agenda

Sometimes a question contains a hidden (or not so hidden) agenda. It may be a loaded question. It may be some other type of trick question. It may be a question containing an accusation – 'How could anyone in good conscience possibly suggest cutting funds for the nursing department?' No matter the method, the question contains a 'hook'. The questioner wants to provoke a certain answer so that he or she can argue with it. The question is just a setup for a fight.

Don't fall for this trap. Instead of launching into an answer, acknowledge your suspicions with responses, such as 'Do you have some thoughts on that?' or 'It sounds like you're expecting me to give you a certain answer. What is it you're trying to get me to say?' Politely expose the hidden agenda and get the questioner to speak about it first.

Putting the question in context

'Isn't it true that you were in Mr Smith's bedroom the night he was found stabbed to death in his bed?' This is known as a loaded question. The question is framed in a way that makes the audience members jump to very specific conclusions that make you look bad. Your response has to broaden their frames of reference. You have to provide the missing information that 'unloads' the question. 'Well, yes, as a police photographer, I did take pictures of the crime scene a few hours after Mr Smith died. That's why I was in his bedroom the night he was stabbed to death.' The meaning of any words or behaviours can be distorted if they're taken out of context. Giving a context to any question that needs one is up to you.

Building a bridge

Watch a politician evade a question in the following example. 'Minister Blowhard, are you going to vote against a tax increase?' 'Well sir, you want to know if I'm going to vote against a tax increase. What you're really asking is how can we get more money into the pockets of more hard-working people. Let me tell you about my 12-step plan for reviving the economy. . .'

The minister has built a bridge. He's constructed a phrase that allows him to move from a question he wants to ignore to a topic he wants to address. In this case, the bridge is, 'What you're really asking is. . .' You can use lots of bridges of this sort, for example:

- ✔ 'It makes much more sense to talk about . . .'

- ✔ 'The real issue is . . .'

- ✔ 'The essential question is . . .'

- ✔ 'What you should be asking is . . .'

- ✔ 'If you look at the big picture, your question becomes . . .'

Use a bridge to move a short distance away from a question you dislike, rather than to evade it completely. You lose credibility when you evade a question. You have to give the appearance of at least attempting to answer.

Dealing with Common Types of Questions

Certain types of questions are designed to put you at a disadvantage. What follows are some questions you must be ready to identify as well as some tips on how to handle them.

- ✔ **The yes or no question:** Don't get trapped by this type of question. ('Is your company going to form an alliance with the Okkie Corporation, yes or no?') Unless you're under oath in court, you're not required to provide a yes or no answer. If the question requires a more complex answer, don't hesitate to say what needs to be said. ('The formation of an alliance between our company and Okkie depends on a number of factors. . .') Does this kind of response evade the question? Not really. It evades *the form of the question* that the questioner is trying to force on you, but your answer does address the question.

- ✔ **The forced choice question:** This is a close relative of the yes or no question. Here, the questioner wants to force you to choose between two alternatives and, like the yes or no question, you're not obligated to do so. Sometimes both alternatives offered are bad. ('Does your plan omit security guards because they're too expensive or because you forgot to include them?' 'Neither. I didn't include them because they're not needed.') Sometimes you just don't want to choose between the alternatives. ('What is the main focus of your growth strategy – developing new products or cutting costs?' 'Actually, we intend to do both of those and more. We will also be acquiring new products, expanding our sales force. . .')

- ✔ **The hypothetical question:** Don't get sucked into the morass of hypothetical questions. ('What if the product doesn't sell up to your expectations?') You've got enough 'real' things to worry about. Just say something like, 'I don't anticipate that happening, so we'll cross that bridge if we come to it.'

- ✔ **The false-assumption question:** The classic example is, 'Have you stopped beating your wife yet?' The question assumes that you've been beating your wife. (And you may not even be married.) False assumptions can also include incorrect facts and statistics, as well as incorrect conclusions that the questioner has drawn from your talk. The solution: Point out the false assumption and correct it immediately.

- ✔ **The multipart question:** 'Could you tell me if we'll be receiving raises this year, and if not, why not, and if so, how big will they be?' Whoa. Slow down there. This is a multipart question. When you get a question like this, divide it up and answer one part at a time.

Responding to Special Situations

Handling questions from the audience is a very delicate situation. You often need to take a firm hand, but you don't want to alienate your listeners. Use the following tips to handle common 'problem' situations.

- ✔ **A questioner interrupts you.** Don't interrupt the interrupter. Stop talking and let this boor finish what he's saying. Then say something like, 'Please wait until I've finished.' Then complete your answer. If the person interrupts again, repeat the process. Don't get into a fight. If the interrupter continues, other members of the audience will eventually intercede on your behalf. (If they don't, then they don't deserve to hear your pearls of wisdom.) And don't let your irritation show on your face.

- ✔ **Someone asks about something you covered in your presentation.** Don't say, 'I already covered that in my talk.' Perhaps you did, but maybe you didn't cover the issue clearly. If the person asking the question missed the answer in your presentation, then others may have missed it, too. And if it was important enough to include in your initial talk, then you can spend time going over it again. So answer the question; just try explaining it in a different way this time.

- ✔ **Someone asks a question that was already asked.** If your answer will take more than ten seconds, politely refuse to answer. Say something like, 'We've already addressed that question.' This situation is completely different from getting a question about something covered in your presentation. Here, the audience member simply hasn't been paying attention. If you answer the question, then you're being rude to the rest of the audience. You're wasting their time. If you want to be nice, offer to talk with the questioner individually after the Q&A session is concluded.

- ✔ **Someone asks a completely irrelevant question.** You can point out gently that their question is not germane to the discussion and go on to the next questioner. You can give the questioner a chance to ask a relevant question, or you can use the question as a springboard to raise a topic you want to discuss.

✔ **Someone asks a completely disorganised question.** You have a couple of choices. You can ask the person to restate the question (not a good idea because you'll probably get a question more disorganised than the first attempt). You can respond to part of the question (a part that you liked), or you can offer to talk with the person individually after the Q&A session is concluded.

✔ **Someone asks a 'techie' question.** 'Why did you change the bitmap for the icons on your menu screen for the financial applications in Release 3.1?' Unless you are dealing with a specialist, 'techie' audience, a 'techie' question may be of interest to only one person in the audience – the questioner. For everyone else the question is a painful distraction. Any time and effort you put into answering it is wasted on the rest of the audience. To handle this situation, after the question is asked, answer it briefly. Then ask for a show of hands to see if anyone else is interested in the topic. If you find significant audience interest, continue your answer. If not, offer to resume the discussion after the Q&A session has concluded. Of course, if you are faced with an audience composed mainly of techies, then by all means get as technical as you like and watch all the little techie faces light up with joy!

✔ **Someone asks multiple questions.** You have a few options for handling this situation. You can tell the questioner that you'll only answer one of the questions due to time constraints and fairness to other audience members. (Offer to answer the other questions later after everyone else has had a turn to ask one.) You can answer all of the questions in the order asked, or you can answer all of them in an order you choose. (Exercise these last two options when you feel that answering the questions is to your advantage.)

✔ **Someone asks a long, rambling question.** If you see where the question is going, gently interrupt (citing time considerations) and pose the question concisely in your own words. Confirm that you've understood what the questioner wants to know. Then answer it. If you don't see where the question's going, ask 'Purely in the interests of time, would you mind stating your question, please?'

Handling Hostile Questions

The prospect of dealing with hostile questions is a huge fear facing many speakers and presenters. Stop worrying. You can use tried-and-tested techniques for handling this problem. In fact, a little advance planning can significantly reduce your chance of receiving these pesky questions altogether.

Identifying hostile questions

Don't put a chip on your shoulder and assume that anyone who disagrees with you is hostile. Even people who disagree can have a legitimate question. They don't necessarily want to argue with you. They may just want information.

However, if someone asks you a false assumption question they are being hostile. ('Do you think you'll get 10 or 20 years for income tax evasion?' and 'Isn't this an amazing achievement – for a woman?') You can safely assume these questioners are out to get you.

Heading them off at the pass

The simplest way to handle hostile questions is to not get any. Unfortunately, we can't guarantee that you won't, but these techniques can help you minimise the number you do receive:

- **The inoculation:** Can you anticipate specific hostile questions that you'll receive? Then raise them and answer them during your presentation. By beating your enemies to it, you leave them with nothing to ask you.

- **The admission:** Admit at the outset of the Q&A session that you're not the world authority on everything. Set audience expectations properly regarding the extent and areas of your expertise. Tell the audience what you don't know. This technique helps defuse potential hostility and disappointment resulting from your inability to answer specific questions.

✔ **The revelation:** At the outset of the Q&A session, announce that the people who ask questions must begin by identifying themselves. They must reveal their name, organisation, and anything else you want to require. Having to reveal this information is a major barrier to hostile questioners. They don't like losing the cloak of audience anonymity. Acting like an idiot, being hostile, and getting confrontational with the speaker is much easier if no one knows who you are.

Dealing with hostile questions

Receiving a hostile question is like being tossed a bomb. You need to know how to defuse it before it blows up in your face. Use the following tactics:

✔ **Empathise with the questioner.** Start by recognising that the questioner is upset and emphasise that you *understand* his or her point of view even if you don't agree with it. Make sure you communicate that you bear no personal animosity toward the questioner. Your disagreement is solely about the issue in question. 'I can see that you feel strongly about this issue, and I understand where you're coming from. Let me give you a few more facts that may affect your opinion. . .'

✔ **Establish common ground.** Find an area where you and the questioner can agree and build your answer from there. 'Then we agree that the budget will have to be limited to 75 per cent of what we spent last year. We just differ on how to allocate the money. . . .' If you're really stuck for finding common ground, the all-purpose (albeit somewhat weak) response that works for any hostile question is: 'Well, at least we agree that this is a controversial issue. . .'

✔ **Put the question in neutral.** If you get a question loaded with emotionally charged words or phrases, rephrase the question in neutral terms. (See the 'Rephrasing the question' section, earlier in this chapter.)

✔ **Be very specific.** Talk about specific facts and figures. Be concrete. The more you get into theory, speculation, and opinion, the more opportunity you provide for disagreement. You want to limit the opportunities for arguments.

✔ **Ask why they're asking.** What if you're on the receiving end of a loaded question or any other blatantly hostile query? Don't even bother giving an answer. Just say, 'May I ask, why did you ask that?' Doing so can go a long way to defusing the situation. The questioner, often embarrassed that you spotted the trap, may withdraw or modify the question. (See the 'Exposing a hidden agenda section, earlier in this chapter.)

✔ **Elude the hostile questioners.** Don't allow continued follow-up questions from people who just want to interrogate you in a hostile manner. No reason exists for it. You should be giving everyone in the audience a chance to ask questions. Just tell them that other people would like a turn to ask questions. You can also say that you'll be happy to discuss their concerns at the conclusion of the Q&A session.

Chapter 14

Handling the Audience

. . . .

. . . .

*Y*ou can have the world's greatest presentation, but that may not mean very much if you have the world's worst audience. An audience is like a thorny, long-stemmed rose. Handled properly, a rose is a thing of beauty that can blossom as you speak. Handled improperly, it will prick you severely.

Reading an Audience's Reaction

Some professional speakers claim they can 'read' an audience like a book. We've always wondered what that means. They read a little of the audience at bedtime, drift off to sleep, and read some more the next day? They mark up the audience with a yellow highlighter? They put a bookmark down the audience's throat? Actually, it makes a lot more sense to read an audience like an audience – a group of people who have to listen to your presentation. What follows are a few ways to gauge their reactions.

Checking the energy level

One of the easiest ways to read an audience is by observing its energy level. Are people talking and laughing as they wait for the event to begin? That behaviour is indicative of a high-energy audience, and that's what you hope for. This type of audience is much more receptive to your presentation. A high-energy audience is basically yours to lose. If you have a high-energy audience, you don't have to be high-energy yourself. (Although it doesn't hurt.)

A high-energy audience laughs and applauds longer than a low-energy audience. Therefore, you need to allow extra time for laughter and applause when you calculate how much you can say in the time you've been allotted.

A low-energy audience is just the opposite. No one's talking, and the mood is kind of so-so. (This mood often correlates to specific times of the day and week. For example, Monday night audiences are typically low-energy.) This audience is tough. You may need to be a bit more energetic to ignite the audience.

Noticing body language

The nonverbal behaviour of your audience can tell you an enormous amount about the effectiveness of your presentation or speech. Are people nodding at what you say? Are they looking up at you? Are they leaning forward? Are they smiling? Or are they squirming in their seats, nudging each other, looking at their watches, and staring out of the windows? (You don't need a PhD to interpret these signals.)

Don't judge the entire audience by the reactions of a single person. This tip sounds obvious, but some speakers do focus on one person and, as a result, come to the wrong conclusions. You may see one person who won't crack a smile. You could become obsessed with this person and make all your speaking decisions based on his or her reaction. Doing so's usually a mistake, because nothing you do will work with the sour-faced individual, and you'll get nervous, feel you're doing a bad job, and screw up. If you look at the other 99 per cent of the audience, you'll see that they're enjoying your talk – at least until you screw it up by focusing only on the one sourpuss in the crowd.

Asking questions to gauge the audience

If you don't know whether people in an audience agree with you, disagree with you, or even understand what you're saying, ask them. Doing so is the direct method of reading audience reaction. ('How many of you are familiar with the large oil spill that I was just talking about?' 'How many of you disagree with what I just said?' 'How many of you have never heard any of these arguments before?')

Putting the Audience at Ease

Most people are cautious in an unfamiliar situation. If they're interacting with a stranger, they assume a conservative demeanour. These people don't let their guards down and kick back until they're sure that doing so's a safe behaviour. Audiences react in much the same way. If the Pope were to step up to a podium, the audience would expect to behave discreetly. If Peter Kay or Dawn French were to step up, the audience knows laughing's okay. If someone the audience doesn't know steps up to the podium, people in the audience don't know how they're expected to behave. You have to tell them.

This process is called *giving permission*. Most of us are strangers in front of crowds. So you have to give the audience permission to enjoy your presentation.

What kind of permissions must audiences receive? The answer depends on what you want to accomplish and how you want the audience to react. The following list shows you three of the more important permissions you can bestow on your listeners:

  ✔ **Permission to laugh:** Do you want to use humour successfully in your talk? One of the most important permissions you can give your audience is the right to laugh. Unless you are a well-known stand-up comedian, your audience may not know that laughing is okay – especially in a business setting. So start by telling your audience it's okay to enjoy themselves. Say something like, 'I intend to communicate and inform and enlighten and bring insight, but it is an explicit goal that you be entertained. I promise you there's a lot of meat in this material, but we also put some fun in with it too.'

✔ **Permission to learn:** You may want to give your audience permission to learn, too. Try saying, 'I believe this is a really important presentation. I'm going to be talking about three sensitive, important topics. I'll go into more detail later. But I think when you leave here today, the things you'll really remember about this talk are these key areas. . . .' By telling the audience the parts that are important, you give them insight into your interpretation of your own talk. Then your audience can actively follow the outline with you – not just react to it as you dump it on them.

✔ **Permission to write:** Many audience members will take notes anyway. But sometimes they don't know if doing so is okay. So state explicitly that you give the audience permission to take notes. Start by saying something like, 'My presentation is packed with information you'll want to remember. That's why I've supplied pencils and paper on your seats. If you don't have some, please make friends immediately with someone who does because you may need them.'

Handling a Tough Audience

Not every audience you ever address will be an absolute delight. When you face a tough crowd, you have some choices. You can figure out the problem and handle it, or you can wait for the twitching and unhappy looks or even aggressive questions and heckling.

Examining types of tough audiences

Easy audiences are all alike, but every tough audience is tough in its own way. Here are some of the varieties you may encounter and some tips for handling each of them.

Bizarre audience

A bizarre audience responds in ways that you don't antici-pate. They laugh or applaud when you don't expect it, and they're silent when you anticipate applause.

The unpredictability is what makes this audience tough. They throw off your entire rhythm. Your only response is to go with the flow. Just don't tell the audience that you find their responses unusual. Pause for their applause when you get it and keep speaking when you don't.

Captive audience

The captive audience is tough because the people aren't there by choice. Attendance at your presentation has been forced upon this audience for one reason or another, and they resent it. So they're in a foul mood before you even begin. The audi-ence's mood isn't your fault. It has nothing to do with you, but you'll have to bear the brunt of their anger. What can you do? Acknowledge the situation up front and appeal to their sense of fairness. Tell them what benefits they can expect to receive if they simply give you a fair chance.

More-educated- or more-experienced-than-you audience

You're presenting on a topic that you know a lot about. But then, uh-oh, you realise that you recognise someone in the audience. In fact, that someone taught you at university. Or that person is your boss's boss, who's been in the industry for longer than you've been wearing long trousers.

What can you do when your audience knows more about your subject than you do? You can reframe your entire presenta-tion as a review of the basics. As an alternative, you may decide to make the talk intensely personal. The presentation becomes a description of *your* feelings, ideas, and reactions regarding the subject matter. Or you can elevate the discus-sion to a higher, 'big picture' level. ('I'm not here to talk about the detail today. Obviously, some of you know a lot more about it than I do. My comments today will examine the major themes of the topic.')

Hostile-to-your-position audience

You're talking about the pros and cons related to a controver-sial issue – drug liberalisation, euthanasia, whether Dale

Winton's tan needs a top up, whatever. Your audience's opinion is the opposite of yours. So you know they'll be hostile to what you have to say. This will be a tough crowd.

The best approach is to try to disarm the audience immediately. Begin by acknowledging that you have a difference of opinion. (And don't apologise for your opinion; you're entitled to it.) Then appeal to the traditional values of fairness, free speech, and dialogue. Let them know that they'll have a chance to air their views after you're finished speaking. ('We are going to disagree on some fundamental issues. But that's why I'm here today – to have a dialogue about the effects of the hole in the ozone layer. If we all believed the same thing, we couldn't have much of a dialogue. And we will have one, because after I'm done speaking, anyone who wishes to express an opinion will have an opportunity to do so. I only ask that you give me a fair chance to make my case without interrupting me. You don't need to let me know how much you disagree with me. I already know.')

Didn't-come-to-see-you audience

The keynote speaker may be the latest business guru who has written a best-selling book on leadership, the latest politician with his own personality cult, or the latest celebrity in the limelight. The audience has come to see them. Unfortunately, the audience has to sit through a few other speakers before they get to hear the main attraction. Even more unfortunate, *you* are one of the speakers that must precede the star turn.

This audience is tough because they want you to be finished before you've even started. You can't do very much about this situation, but you may find some relief by referring to the keynote speaker in your remarks a handful of times. Doing so may be the only thing you can say to get a positive response from the audience. ('I'm honoured to be here today, presenting at the same event as Mr Guru. In fact, many of my ideas have been influenced directly by Mr Guru's work. How many of you would agree with me that Mr Guru's book *Babble Your Way to Leadership* is the most important business book of the century? Later on today, you'll hear Mr Guru speak about leadership. But right now I'd like to discuss a few concepts that will give you a deeper insight into Mr Guru's ideas.') Is this pandering to the audience? Of course it is. Do you have any other choice? Yes. You can give your presentation as planned to the accompaniment of audience hoots and jeers. ('Hey, shut up and sit down.' 'Get off the stage.' 'We want the Guru.') Take your pick.

The-current-event-distracted-them audience

You're presenting to a group of fundraisers about new techniques to increase donations, and you're an expert on the topic. This situation is a perfect match between speaker, topic, and audience. Your audience should pay undivided attention and take notes, but they aren't. They seem distracted; they're definitely not listening. What is the audience's problem? Two hours before you started speaking, a tsunami devastated most of East Asia, some country has invaded some other country, or the Prime Minister was shot. Some major event has usurped the consciousness of the audience, and everything else – especially your presentation – seems unimportant by comparison.

The distracting event need not be national in scope. It may be very local. In fact, the event may be specific to your audience. (You're scheduled to give a lunch presentation about investment opportunities to a group of employees from Plod-Tech, plc. That morning, Plod-Tech's CEO projects a record quarterly loss and indicates that massive layoffs will be forthcoming. Plod-Tech employees will *not* be focusing on your talk.)

What if you're scheduled to present on the day that a distracting event has occurred? Try to get your presentation cancelled or changed to another time. If neither is possible, be prepared to talk about the distracting event because that may be the only subject that interests your audience.

Reverse-image audience

You're the only man at a women's event or vice versa. You're the only Asian at an Afro-Caribbean event or vice versa. You're the only Christian at a Jewish event or vice versa.

You get the idea. You're the reverse image of your audience. An audience can be tough if they assume that you can't possibly understand their point of view. After all, you're different from them.

Start by breaking the tension. Acknowledge your difference. If appropriate, poke fun at it. Then establish your common ground. You're speaking to this audience for a reason. Members of the audience can receive some benefit from listening to you. Let them know what it is – fast.

Angry-at-previous-speaker audience

The speaker before you has really annoyed the audience. In fact, they're downright livid. Maybe the speaker was controversial. Maybe he was insulting. Maybe he was offensive. Whatever the case, the audience members are in a vile mood, and they want to take it out on you. In this situation, the most important thing you can do is *be aware of it*. You need to know that the audience is angry at the prior speaker, not you.

Failure to recognise this situation can jeopardise your entire presentation. You'll assume that *you* are the problem and adjust your performance accordingly. Doing so doesn't work because you're *not* the problem. You really need to know what any previous speakers said to your audience. Attend their presentations if possible. If not, find out what happened. If a problem occurred, you can address it immediately in the opening of your talk.

Already-heard-it audience

The speakers before you have made acceptable presentations. They left the audience in decent shape for your talk. The audience isn't angry or upset about anything. But that can change rapidly if you get up and repeat what the previous speakers have already said.

Why would anyone do that? This situation happens all the time, and two major causes exist. You may be unaware of what the previous speakers said. Or despite the fact that you know they've already said what you planned to say, you plow ahead with your prepared remarks anyway. Audiences absolutely hate this occurrence. (Repetition is why so many people try to avoid all-day business conferences. When the fifth speaker in a row gets up and talks about the importance of synergy, commitment to change, and the globalisation of business, you just want to vomit.)

If you find yourself in this situation, don't just do your presentation as if the audience haven't already heard the same thing.

You'll lose them instantly. You have to adapt. At a minimum, you have to acknowledge that you'll be saying things that the audience have already heard. A much more effective strategy is to abandon your prepared remarks entirely. Just wing it. Think of a different angle and speak about it on an impromptu basis. Comment on what the previous speakers have already said. Or solicit participation from the audience. (See Chapter 15 for tips on how to deal with impromptu presentations or speeches.)

The best way to avoid repeating material from other speakers' presentations is to talk to your contact who invited you to the event. Try to get as much information as you can about the other speakers' talks so that you can ensure that yours covers different topics or perhaps just different aspects of the same topic.

Unwell audience

The unwell audience is literally ill. Numerous members of this audience cough and sneeze loudly throughout your presentation. The noise is quite a distraction, but you can't do much about it. You can try using humour to deal with the situation. ('Please hold your applause and coughing till the end.') If doing so doesn't work, you're out of luck. Just try to speak more loudly so that other audience members can hear over the coughing.

Haggling with hecklers

The traditional notion of a heckler is someone who interrupts a speaker by shouting out hostile remarks or questions. We're going to define heckling a little more broadly. Our definition of heckling is anything that someone does to purposely distract you or the audience from your presentation. You may encounter some of the following hecklers:

- ✔ **The one-upper:** This person is a heckler who wants attention. If you ask the audience for questions, the one-upper will jump in with some sarcastic comment or tough question designed to embarrass you. The one-upper doesn't dislike you personally or even disagree with your position. You're just a prop for them to manipulate in an unending quest for attention.

- ✔ **The under-the-influence heckler:** If you present at enough dinner meetings, you'll eventually run into an under-the-influence heckler. This person has had a few too many and exhibits the typical effects of alcohol (or drugs) – they get very angry, sad, or happy. Whichever mood it is, this heckler displays it to an exaggerated degree. They shout or cry or laugh in a way that completely disrupts your presentation.

- ✔ **The attack dog:** This person is the traditional heckler. They don't like you or your opinions and are determined to stop you from speaking. He or she will try to shout you down, insult you, and do whatever it takes to cause a commotion. This heckler wants to fight – with you.

Although technically not a heckler, you may run into the 'idiot' at some time. The idiot is someone who unintentionally engages in distracting behaviour related to your discussion, such as answering rhetorical questions. Just be prepared: They don't know any better.

Just because someone causes a distraction doesn't mean they're heckling you. Although hecklers consciously choose to cause a distraction, sometimes distracting behaviour is innocent. For example, a person may be asking a neighbour for a pen to take notes. Or someone may decide to take a call on their mobile. Don't become offended by such unintended distractions. If someone runs out of the room to go to the toilet, you haven't been heckled. If they come back and throw toilet paper at you, that's another story.

Now that you know what types of hecklers you may be facing, here are some pointers on how to deal with them:

- ✔ **Identify the type of heckler.** You need to know why the heckling started so you can determine how you'll end it. See the advice earlier in this section for more information on the types of hecklers and their motives.

- ✔ **Be empathic.** Sometimes you can defuse hecklers just by acknowledging their point of view. Let them know that you understand their position, even if you don't agree with it.

- ✔ **Suggest that the heckler speak with you after your presentation.** Try saying, 'I would like to debate the topic with you and you're more than welcome to come and find me after my presentation. But right now, you're insulting the rest of the audience.'

✔ **Look for help.** You shouldn't have to deal with audience members who are out of control. Seek help from the person running the meeting or the person who invited you to present. You can also appeal to the audience for assistance. 'Perhaps I can refer your comment to the rest of the audience . . .' (Let them tell the heckler to shut up.)

✔ **Avoid arguing.** Doing so just gives legitimacy to the heckler and makes you look bad. And the heckler wants you to do just that.

✔ **Stay calm.** Hecklers want control. If you get angry, you give them exactly what they want – a negative reaction (and confirmation that you've lost control). So stay calm at all times. If nothing else, your serenity will drive the heckler nuts.

✔ **Discontinue the rest of your presentation**. If the heckler won't stop and no one will help you, then end your talk. Tell the audience that you can't proceed due to the disruption. Apologise to the rest of them. Then exit gracefully.

Dealing with other distractions

Hecklers are (thankfully) a rare occurrence at most presentations; other distractions are far more common. If you're speaking at a lunch or dinner, a waiter will inevitably drop some dishes during your talk. If there are children present, a baby will cry. The audience member with the loudest ringing mobile phone will receive a call (and then proceed to take it – loudly) while you're speaking. The list goes on.

When these types of distractions occur, an audience often reacts with laughter. If that occurrence happens, you have to laugh along with the audience. Doing so's a control issue. You have to show the audience that you're handling the problem and that you remain in control. (This response is analogous to skidding while driving a car. If you steer into the skid, you regain control.) If you get upset about the distraction, the audience becomes uncomfortable, and you lose momentum.

Heckling the hecklers

The greatest nightmare for many speakers is the prospect of being interrupted by a heckler. But don't overlook the fact that being heckled provides a great opportunity for you to respond with wit and acumen. In fact, a good retort is usually remembered long after the actual presentation is forgotten. Below are some examples.

William Gladstone and Benjamin Disraeli were archrivals in Parliament. During one of their many debates, Gladstone yelled at Disraeli, 'You, sir, will die either on the gallows or of some loathsome disease.' Disraeli responded, 'That, sir, depends upon whether I embrace your principles or your mistress.'

Nancy Astor, the first woman to sit in the House of Commons, was an outspoken proponent of women's rights. During one of her speeches on the subject, a heckler interrupted with comments about Lady Astor's numerous bracelets and necklace. The heckler said, 'You have enough brass on you, Lady Astor, to make a kettle.' Astor's reply was quick and devastating: 'And you have enough water in your head to fill it.'

Anticipate things that can go wrong and have some quips ready to deal with them. For example, assume the room lights go out because of a power failure. You might say, 'Now I'm really going to have to shed some light on the subject.' (No, this response isn't hilarious, but it doesn't have to be. It communicates that you're not upset and that you're still in control.)

Handling a Nonresponsive Audience

You can pick up subtle clues that tell you when you're not clicking with an audience. (People don't nod in agreement, but they do nod off.) If you want to save your presentation, then you have to take charge. Your speaking engagement is like working in a casualty department. You need to figure out what's wrong with the patients, but first you have to revive them – before it's too late. Here are some resuscitation techniques for nonresponsive audiences.

Stocking your first-aid kit

An audience first-aid kit includes a variety of devices for reviving interest in your presentation. Like the contents of a real first-aid kit, these devices range in strength from bandages to adrenaline. You have to know how to use the appropriate device for the audience in front of you. You may find it helpful to diagnose a dying audience by sorting it into one of three categories, which we'll refer to as levels.

Level one: You still have the audience's attention, but they look bored or puzzled

The people in the audience are still watching you present, but you can sense that you're not connecting. They're fidgeting. They're not responding. What can you do? You must break out of the pattern you're in. Talk directly to the audience as though you're having a real conversation. Ask them if they understand what you're talking about. Ask if they'd like you to give another example. Or tell them that what you're about to say is very important. Emphasise a key benefit that really puts them in the picture. ('Now I'd like to tell you the only guaranteed way to prevent yourself from being laid off in the next two years.')

Or you can say something that you feel is guaranteed to get applause. (The energy of their hands clapping helps prevent the onset of lethargy.) What if you're waiting for applause and you don't get it? Say something like, 'Oh, I guess you didn't think that was as important as I did.' If they laugh, you've connected with them. If they don't, you're not any worse off.

 A risky (but sometimes effective) tactic to maximise your chances of getting applause is to ask the audience some questions and tell them to respond with applause instead of a show of hands. ('How many of you can't wait until my presentation is finished?' Thundering ovation.)

Level two: Audience attention is waning

The audience is starting to drift off. People are staring at the ceiling, out of the windows, and at their watches. The only thing they're not looking at is you. One of the simplest things you can do to revive this audience is also one of the most effective – just ask them to stand up. Say something like, 'I'm going to ask you some questions, and I'd like you to stand up if you have experienced this in the last 18 months. Who's had an argument with a colleague?' Or try, 'You've been sitting down for a while now. And I think we could all use a short stretch. Everyone stand up. . . . Okay, sit back down. Feel better?' A stretch can really transform the energy level in the room. But let us add a word of caution. The effect is temporary. When the audience retake their seats, they pay attention for a minute or two. That period is your chance to get your presentation back on track with some exciting, dynamic stuff. If you don't, you'll lose the audience again.

Level three: They're about to become comatose

The audience is falling asleep or in a trancelike state or just plain dazed. You don't have time to ask them to stand up or applaud. You need to do something immediately that will jar the audience out of their stupor. Your action must be loud or dramatic or both. Consider these shock tactics:

- Pound your fist on the podium
- Beat your chest like a gorilla
- Move the mike toward a sound-system speaker to cause loud feedback (just like a gig by The Jesus And Mary Chain)
- Wave a £20 note in the air and then rip it up
- Throw your notes on the floor
- Set the podium on fire

Any of these actions should wake up the audience. But you need to tie these actions into your speech so that they make a point. Otherwise, your behaviour looks like you were just trying to wake the audience up. (You can't admit that your goal was to wake them up. They would resent that. The situation has to appear that you were just giving your talk and part of it happened to revive them.)

For example, you pound your fist on the podium. (Do this action near the mike so it really makes a loud noise.) Then you tie it into whatever you're talking about. 'That's the sound of people beating their head against a wall because they're frustrated with government policy.' 'That's the sound of your heart beating when you go to a job interview.' 'That's the sound your car makes after you try to save £150 by going to the non-VAT registered mechanic.'

Getting a volunteer from the audience

One of the best ways to coax a response out of an audience is to put one of them into your act. This tactic's an ego thing. The audience identifies with the person who stands before them. Suddenly your talk becomes a lot more personal.

Meeting members of your audience before you speak helps you get a volunteer. Whenever we've had to beg for a volunteer, the person who came forward has always been someone we've spoken with earlier. Why does this happen? Your guess is as good as ours. Maybe some kind of bonding takes place. The person now feels like we're friends and feels obligated to help out. Who knows? We can only tell you that this scenario happens consistently.

Part V
Common Speaking Situations

'Escape plan in operation – pass it on!'

In this part . . .

*H*ey, we live in the information age. Presentations and public speaking are just one of the ways that information is communicated. So, whether or not you speak on a regular basis, most people can expect to be called on to give a speech now and then – sometimes even at the last minute. In this part of the book, we describe common speaking situations and how to handle them, situations including everything from giving an impromptu speech, participating in a panel discussion, introducing other speakers, and presenting to international audiences in the global workplace.

Chapter 15

Giving Impromptu Talks and Introducing Other Speakers

· ·

In This Chapter

▶ Making an impromptu speech

▶ Giving the introduction for other presenters

· ·

*W*hen people think about presentations and public speaking, they usually imagine someone standing alone in front of an audience, delivering a carefully prepared speech. But speaking in public can include so much more than that. You may have to give a talk off the top of your head. Or you may have to introduce another speaker. In this chapter, you find out how to successfully handle both situations.

Saying a Few Words: Giving Impromptu Talks

'Say a few words.' This phrase can strike terror into the heart of the bravest soul. But view this request as an opportunity. Really. Everyone knows that you had no time to prepare, so no one expects you to deliver a speech on the level of orators such as Winston Churchill or Martin Luther King. You're held to a much lower standard – wherein lies the opportunity. If you say anything remotely well organised and intelligent, you'll be perceived as a genius.

Of course, you can do a few things to help you succeed. The first is to realise that you're not likely to be asked to give an impromptu talk unless you know about the subject. So you really do have a good head start. The second is to be ready when you're asked. The following sections ensure you'll be as prepared as possible for your next impromptu talk.

Being prepared

Yes, the whole idea of an impromptu talk is that you don't know that you'll be asked to speak. But that doesn't mean you can't *anticipate* the possibility. Watch the BAFTAs or the glitzy Academy Awards. Only one person wins best actor, but five nominees have acceptance speeches sticking out of their pockets. Take a cue from the professionals: Be ready to speak.

How can you anticipate when you may be asked to share your wisdom? Use your common sense. Are you going to an event honouring a friend, colleague, or relative? Assuming that you may be asked to make a toast or utter a few words of praise isn't a big leap.

Are you going to a business meeting? Take a look at the agenda? It may suggest topics you'd better be prepared to discuss – even if you're *not* a scheduled speaker. Think about the issues that may arise. Would you need to respond to any of them?

Buying time

Nothing makes time pass faster than holidays, credit card debts, and being asked to give an impromptu talk. The time between 'can you say a few words' and when you start talking can go by faster than a speeding bullet. Yet this time is crucial to the success of your impromptu remarks. You need it to plan and organise your entire talk.

Your goal is to lengthen this time period as much as possible. Do it any way you can. Use the following ideas to get started.

Pause thoughtfully

When someone asks you to say a few words, you're not required to immediately start talking. You can pause and think. This technique actually increases your credibility. The audience assumes that your words are now carefully considered rather than the first thoughts that flew into your head. (Little do they know.) You can even use some showmanship.

Tilt your head slightly to one side. Furrow your brow. Squint a bit. Let the audience know that they're in the presence of some incredibly powerful thinking.

Repeat the question

This technique is the traditional stalling device, but a good reason exists to use it aside from gaining more time. Knocking yourself out giving a fabulous impromptu talk is pointless if it turns out to be on the wrong subject. Put the question in your own words. Then get confirmation that you've stated it correctly.

Be ready with an all-purpose quote

Memorising a few all-purpose quotes doesn't hurt – lines that you can use to begin *any* impromptu talk. Quoting someone makes you sound clever, and you gain a little extra time to think about what you really want to say. For example, if you need to toast someone or talk up the qualities of just about anybody or anything, consider the following:

> 'Oscar Wilde once said: "A little sincerity is a dangerous thing, and a great deal of it is absolutely fatal." However, I find it very easy to be sincere about [insert your topic here].'

Just make sure that you don't keep using the same quote over and over again for every event – people are bound to recognise it and start to roll their eyes – 'Oh not that old chestnut again . . .'

Organising your thoughts

When you know you have to give a talk in 20 seconds, you definitely need to concentrate your mind. Here are some tips for organising what you're going to say.

Make a quick decision

The big myth with impromptu speaking is that your mind goes blank as soon as you're asked to speak. Actually, the opposite happens. Most people get an overwhelming number of ideas, and almost any of them will do the job. You need to pick one idea and stick with it. The secret of an impromptu talk is to commit to one main point – quickly.

Pick a pattern

After you select your main point, you have to organise your talk. What are your subpoints? How will you support them? Do you have examples or anecdotes? You need to pick a pattern of organisation – something that allows you to quickly sort out your information. The following are two popular approaches:

- ✔ **Organise around the conclusion.** Decide on a conclusion. Organise all your information so that it supports your conclusion. Then start speaking. Everything you say should be designed to move your message toward the conclusion you select.

- ✔ **Organise around a standard pattern.** Pick one of the standard speech patterns – past, present, future, problem, solution, cause and effect – and quickly fit its structure to your message (see Chapter 4 for more on different patterns). Many speakers find the chronological pattern easiest to use.

Find an opening

You can begin an impromptu talk in many ways. But if the audience don't know that you're speaking off the cuff, then you have only one way to begin – tell them. Make absolutely sure that they know. Otherwise, the audience applies a higher standard to your remarks. And when you're speaking off the cuff, you don't want to be judged as if you had months to prepare.

For example, you might say, 'Because I've just been asked to speak and haven't had time to prepare, I may not cover the topic as thoroughly as I usually do. So please let me know if you have any questions when I'm done.'

Usually, however, the audience realises that your talk is impromptu. So you can choose one of the following ways to begin:

- ✔ **Tie into previous speakers.** This is probably the easiest opening. You just react to what's already been said.

- ✔ **Be candid.** If you really don't know much about the subject, admit that you're not an expert. Then offer whatever information you can contribute to the discussion. If you're completely clueless, offer to gather information and provide it in the future.

✔ **Tell a personal anecdote.** Think of a story relevant to the issue at hand and which makes your point. 'That reminds me of the time I worked at Company X. We faced a similar issue. . . .'

✔ **Switch the topic.** This method is popular with politicians. They're asked for their opinion on a tax increase, and they give their opinion on something else.

One final word of advice on openings. Never apologise. What would you apologise for anyway? Not having a carefully polished presentation ready? You're giving an impromptu talk! By definition, what you say is off the cuff.

Stop talking

Keep it brief and stop when you're finished. This advice sounds obvious – but most people don't follow it. Rambling is the most common mistake related to impromptu speaking. To avoid this problem you need to know where you're going. Make sure that you think about a conclusion in the short time you have to organise your thoughts. Then stick to your plan. When you get to the conclusion – stop.

Introducing Other Presenters

A common task you may be called upon for is introducing other speakers. If you're tapped for this duty, a special set of rules applies. When you introduce speakers, you need to say who they are and what they'll talk about. But you also need to do several other things. A good introduction should warm up the audience and get them excited about the speaker. It should set a positive tone for the event, and it shouldn't discourage the speaker from speaking. (Most speakers are nervous enough without the added pressure of a lousy introduction.)

If you're asked to introduce someone, take the time to do a good job. The better you make the speaker look, the better you make yourself look.

Checklist of speaker interview questions

Interviewing the person you're introducing is probably the best way to get the material you need. Choose whichever of the following questions you think are relevant to get your interview started:

- ✔ Why are you giving your talk?

- ✔ What do you want to accomplish with your talk?

- ✔ What is your expertise regarding the topic of your talk?

- ✔ How did you get interested in your topic?

- ✔ Whom should I contact to get some good stories about you?

- ✔ What are the two or three most important things for the audience

to know about you? What are the two or three most important things for the audience to know about your talk?

- ✔ Do you belong to any interesting groups or organisations? Have you worked for any big or impressive companies that should be mentioned?

- ✔ Do you have any hobbies?

- ✔ Is there anything that you specifically do or don't want me to mention?

- ✔ Is there anything you thought I was going to ask or that I should have asked you?

Finding information about the speaker

Information is the key to making an appropriate introduction. The introduction you do will only be as good as the information you get. And that can be a problem, especially if all you have to work with is a speaker's official company biography.

Find out if any other written material about the speaker exists. Was she profiled in a company or association newsletter? Was he written up in the local paper? Your goal is to get *too much* information. Then you can pick and choose the best stuff.

No written materials? Don't worry. You can interview the speaker. Interview people who know the speaker. (Or interview people who used to know the speaker. One of the most interesting introductions we've ever heard included quotes from one of the speaker's old girlfriends.) If you need to make a lengthy introduction, try to talk to the speaker's friends, relatives, and colleagues. Talk to the speaker's clients and customers. You'll get good stories and quotes from these people.

Making a speaker (and yourself) look good

The way that you introduce other speakers says as much about you as it does about them. The following tips ensure that you both come out looking good.

Make the introduction interesting

Anyone can get a speaker's CV, stand at a podium, and read it. But this introduction's boring and is a disservice to both the speaker and your audience. Reading a CV means that you didn't take the time to put together an introduction that sets a great tone and whets the crowd's appetite for the main event.

Make the speaker real. Quote the speaker. Tell some anecdotes about the speaker. Let the audience see the speaker as a human being – not a CV.

Don't ignore the speaker's accomplishments though. Pick out a few of the major ones and show how they relate to the speaker's topic. The audience wants to know what the speaker will talk about and why he or she is qualified. So tell them.

Get the speaker's name right

Nothing is more embarrassing than mispronouncing the name of the person you're introducing. You lose a lot of credibility if you get the name wrong and appear sloppy, silly, and unprepared. Make sure you ask the speaker for the correct pronunciation!

Keep the introduction brief

The introduction should be short and sweet. If you're introducing a head of state or similar dignitary, maybe you can go
as long as three to four minutes. (And that length of time's
really pushing the limit.) For anyone else, one to two minutes
is plenty.

Co-ordinate with the person you're introducing

Check the information you use in the introduction with the
person you're introducing. Make sure all the information is
correct and find out if the speaker wants anything *omitted*.

Talk to the audience

The person doing the introduction gets to the podium, takes
out some notes, and gives the introduction. But she only looks
at the speaker she's introducing. Doing so's a common mistake. Don't make it. When you introduce someone, look at the
audience. Even if you're reading the introduction word for
word, when you look up from your notes, look at the audience.

Announce if there'll be a question-and-answer session

The audience wants to know when it can ask questions. Is
there going to be a Q&A session after the speaker's presentation? Or do audience members have to chase the speaker
after the presentation on an individual basis? Either way, if
you let the audience know about the Q&A protocol in the
introduction, you save the speaker the chore.

Avoiding introduction errors

Sometimes the easiest way to do something right is by not
doing anything wrong. The following guidelines help you
avoid common introduction errors.

- ✔ **Don't give the speaker's presentation.** You're supposed
  to announce what the speaker will talk about, but that's
  all. Don't go into minute detail about what the speaker
  will cover – or there'll be nothing left for them to cover.

- ✔ **Don't give your own presentation.** Again, you're just
  supposed to announce what the speaker will talk about.
  While your views on the subject may be fascinating, no
  one came to hear them. Holding a microphone is not a
  licence to give a talk. Get on with the intro and get off.

✔ **Don't over-promise.** You want to get the audience excited about the speaker and the topic – but not over-excited. Raising the audience's expectations too much makes things tougher for the speaker. If you say that the speaker is a brilliant orator who will make the audience laugh while tugging at their heartstrings and changing their lives, you're setting the speaker up for a fall. Give a good build-up, but don't go crazy.

✔ **Don't gush.** We don't know who gets more embarrassed by a gushing introduction – the person being introduced or the audience. Either way, the person doing the introduction looks ridiculous. Yes, you're supposed to praise the speaker, but don't go overboard.

✔ **Don't wing it.** You did a lot of research. You have some great stories about the speaker. You edited the speaker's list of achievements down to the ones relevant to the audience. Don't blow it now by winging it. Write out the introduction and stick to it.

Chapter 16

Handling Panels and Roundtables

*B*eing on a panel or taking part in a roundtable discussion – each poses a unique challenge. Yet many people come to these types of engagements unprepared. Why? They don't consider these situations to be as challenging as presenting or public speaking and they don't know how to prepare for them. In this chapter, we not only point out the challenges you may face, but we also show you how to overcome them.

Being on a Panel

Many people who don't enjoy giving presentations say they would rather speak as part of a panel than as a sole presenter. Panelists usually don't have to speak for the same length of time as a sole presenter, and they can pass tough audience questions to other panelists. Of course, if you're ready for the unique challenges that the panel format presents, you'll shine. If you're not, you'll get ignored and quickly forgotten.

Winning the inevitable comparison

Compared with a sole presenter, panelists have much less control over their message and image because the audience *compares* panelists to each other as they speak. To strategise for your panel session, ask yourself the following questions.

Who else is on the panel?

Finding out who else is on your panel sounds pretty obvious, and it is. But, amazingly, many people don't bother to check. Finding out who else is on your panel is necessary. How can you influence the audience's comparison if you don't know who you'll be compared to?

Find out everything you can about the other panelists: their names, qualifications, jobs, knowledge of the topic, reputations as speakers, and so on. And don't forget to ask about the moderator, facilitator, or chairperson. Is there one? If so, you want to know everything about this person, too.

What are the rules?

Every panel operates within some set of rules. You need to know those rules. Does everyone on the panel make his or her remarks before the audience asks questions? Or does the audience ask questions after each panelist speaks? Are the panelists even expected to make remarks? How much time is allotted for the entire session? How much time is given to each panelist? Is there a moderator, or is it a free-for-all? What's the physical setup? Does each panelist have a microphone, or do the panelists have to pass one around? Whether you want to follow them, bend them, or break them, you have to know the rules.

What is the speaking order?

The order in which panelists speak is a major factor in determining how you're perceived. Think about these factors:

> ✔ **First speaker:** The advantage of going first is that you can't be compared to anyone – yet. So, if you're on a panel with several strong speakers, going first makes a lot of sense. Another advantage is that the first speaker can set the tone for the entire panel. Go first, give a well-structured talk, and

you set the standard. The audience now expects the other speakers to do at least as well as you did. The disadvantage of going first is that you can't react to the other panelists. They haven't said anything yet.

✔ **Last speaker:** The biggest advantage of going last is that you can comment on what all of the other panelists have said. This allows you to have the final word in defining the discussion. Going last is also the best position if you're not prepared. You can formulate your remarks while the earlier panelists are speaking, and you can comment on what they just said.

✔ **Middle speaker:** The advantage of going in the middle is that you can comment on any panelists that spoke before you, and you can still shape the discussion of the panelists that go after you. The disadvantage is that you may get lost in the shuffle. Psychologists have defined the 'primacy' and 'recency' effects – that people most strongly remember things that come first or last. In a panel situation, that means what the first and the last speaker said.

What other things should you consider?

How big is the panel? What time of day does the session occur? The answers to these questions may affect your choice of when you want to speak (if you have a choice). A large panel with many speakers increases the chance that the audience is burned out by the time the last speaker gets a turn. The slot just after lunch is often called the 'graveyard' slot because the audience may be feeling a tad sleepy after their lunch. A panel held in the late afternoon means that the audience won't be focused on the last speaker (except for wondering when he or she will end so that everyone can go to dinner). With a very early morning panel, the audience may still be waking up while the first panelist is speaking. If you can, try to pick what suits you.

Maintaining control of your message

Panel discussions create special obstacles to getting your message across the way you desire. You want to maintain as much control as possible. Paying attention to the following factors helps you achieve that goal.

Knowing why you're on the panel

Your answer to this question shapes your message strategy. Are you on the panel as a favour to the moderator? Are you there to showcase yourself and your ideas? Are you there to gain recognition for your company or organisation? Who, if anyone, are you trying to impress? You need to know what you want to accomplish.

Preparing your message

Any speech requires you to decide how you'll get the audience to remember your key messages. This goal is even more challenging in a panel discussion because a lot is going on. The audience is bombarded by messages from your co-panelists. And the audience itself may offer statements or questions that provide further distraction from your key ideas. Your messages have a lot of competition, so you have to make them powerful, persuasive, and to the point.

Start by finding out who the audience members are. What organisations do they represent? What are their jobs? What positions do they hold? You can involve them in your remarks by speaking directly to their interests, and then they don't have to wait for the Q&A session to get involved.

Anticipate where you'll be challenged on particular issues. You don't want co-panelists or the audience to sink your entire message by torpedoing you on one point – especially if you anticipate being challenged on that issue. Defuse the situation by addressing the issue in your remarks before the Q&A session.

 Listen to the other panelists. We mean really listen. Be prepared to refer back to specific things they said. This tip is especially effective if you get the panelists' names right ('As Heather and Amy said earlier . . .').

Getting the timing right

Panelists get many opportunities to present information, such as when they make their remarks, answer questions from co-panelists, answer audience questions, and even when they tag statements onto the end of co-panelists' answers to audience questions. But not all opportunities to present information are equally useful. Depending on what you want to say, certain times to say it are better than others.

If you have important information for the audience, don't convey it straight away. Let them settle down first and get used to the panelists. And don't wait until the end as you may run out of time, or the audience may be distracted by their preparations to leave. Key information is best presented after the audience has heard you for a few minutes or a few times.

Another aspect of timing has to do with whom the audience credits with an idea. Credit may not always be given to the panelist who smentioned the idea first. More often, the panelist who talks about an idea second is given credit – the' one who takes the idea and runs with it. This second panelist expands the idea, puts it into new words, and makes it his or her own. The audience don't always remember that someone else mentioned the idea first. Keep this in mind when you toss your gems into the discussion. If your idea's a diamond in the rough, don't wait for a fellow panelist to polish it.

Timing also applies to how much you speak. If you speak every time a question or issue is raised, you seem pompous, and your answers lose their impact. People stop listening to you. But if you never speak up, you seem weak and irrelevant – if the audience even remembers you're there. So monitor yourself. Be aware of how much time you spend speaking. Assert yourself but don't go wild.

Planning your delivery

If you get into a debate with another panelist, you may easily forget about the audience. Doing so's a mistake. The majority of your eye contact and 'face time' should be with the audience. Focus on different sections of the room as you answer different questions. Make everyone feel like you're talking to him or her.

Don't become a victim of microphone placement. If only one mike is provided for all the panelists, make sure that you have access to it. And please, don't lean forward to use it. Lift the microphone up and bring it toward your mouth. Too many speakers seem like they're bowing at the altar of the microphone. This piece of equipment isn't a deity. You should control it – not the other way around.

Interacting with other panelists

Your interaction with other panelists has a major effect on how the audience perceives you. Everyone assumes that panelists will have disagreements. (Otherwise, the panel would be fairly boring.) But *how* you disagree is the important point. So here are two words of advice: Be diplomatic.

If you want to point out an inaccuracy stated by another panelist, say something like, 'I understand how Matt's experience could lead to his conclusion. However, I have found that. . .' Don't say that Matt is an idiot. The audience will get the idea.

You should also know where to turn for help. Which panelists are your allies? Which of them support your positions? If you're going to be the first person to take a certain position, you need to know who to turn to for confirmation. And you've got to encourage them to provide it by using two methods. Nonverbally, you can turn to your supporter, establish eye contact, and put him or her on the spot to offer their verbal support. Verbally, you can prompt your supporter by saying something like, 'Matt, haven't you found what I've said to be true?' The main point is this: Don't leave it up to chance. Don't just make your statement and hope someone jumps in to support it. Make the effort to ensure that they do jump in.

Answering questions when you don't get any

Answering questions from the audience is prime time for a panelist. This point is your chance to shine. But what if the other panelists get all the questions? What if none are directed to you? Don't worry – you just need to play tag. As other panelists finish their answers, you can tag on your own statement: 'I'd like to add one thing to what Sam just said. . .' Is this tactic aggressive? Yes. But your jumping in is better than sitting around after the session is over wishing someone had asked you something. To make an impression, you need to have your say.

Dealing with a moderator

We have good news and bad news about panel moderators, facilitators, and chairpersons. The good news is that a good moderator can make the panel a pleasure. The bad news is that a lot of moderators are clueless. They see their function solely as introducing the panel members. When hassles occur –

inappropriate questions from the audience, a scrummage among the panelists – the moderator is nowhere to be found. And sometimes they even screw up the introductions.

You may be better off assuming that moderators will be incompetent – you can celebrate if they're not. Assuming that position means you must be prepared – to reintroduce yourself to the audience; to take charge if other panelists hog your time; and to grab the microphone. And if you get a good moderator who runs a tight ship, be prepared to finish on time.

Having a secret weapon ready

Smart panelists carry a secret weapon in reserve – the *sound bite*. A sound bite's a short line or phrase designed to capture audience attention. The name comes from the radio and television news business. A reporter interviews someone for an hour. That night on the news, you hear the person for 30 seconds – you get the sound bite.

Prepare some sound bites that you can use to support your arguments. Think of them as pithy comments or slogans that you can repeat a couple of times to help the audience remember you. Try saying stuff like 'people win business, not products' or 'you never get a second chance to make a first impression'. Just like catchy advertising slogans, these sound bites are more likely to register in your audience's mind than lengthy spiels or explanations.

Participating in a Roundtable

Another speaking format – closely related to the panel – is the roundtable discussion. And no, an actual round table isn't necessary, and you probably won't witness King Arthur rising from his grave to attend the session.

Figuring out the roundtable format

Like a panel, a roundtable has multiple participants and a moderator. But a roundtable discussion is less formal, encourages interaction between participants, and doesn't require an audience.

A roundtable discussion is best described as a guided conversation. Participants, selected for their expertise, discuss a particular topic or topics. And, as the term *roundtable* suggests, participants are seated so that they all face each other. (Often a rectangular table is used. The point is that all participants can take part in the discussion.)

The participants' conversation is guided by a moderator who facilitates the discussion and keeps the agenda moving. The moderator's responsibilities include beginning and ending the discussion on time; making introductions; keeping the participants on topic; and summarising the discussion. The moderator also makes sure that each participant gets an opportunity to speak.

The format is fairly flexible, but in most roundtable discussions, a moderator introduces the issue under discussion. Then each person on the roundtable takes it in turn to introduce themselves and make a comment. If you can, try to get hold of a copy of the agenda before the roundtable so that you can think about the issues in advance.

The other big difference between a panel and a roundtable is how they're structured. Panelists direct semi-formal remarks to an audience. Roundtable participants direct their remarks to each other and are encouraged to ignore the audience – or they may not even have an audience. The purpose of a roundtable is for experts to have a conversation that may yield insights into the topics under discussion, so an audience may be inappropriate.

Starring in a roundtable discussion

Although roundtable participants are usually chosen for their expertise, the term 'expert' is relative. You don't have to be a brain surgeon or rocket scientist to be an expert. Roundtable discussions can cover everything from neighbourhood improvements to school fundraising ideas. When you're asked to participate in a roundtable, bear these tips in mind:

✔ **Have a few talking points prepared**. Often, the people who are most prepared get to participate most in the discussion. Try to write down three or four points that you want to make before the roundtable begins. Then you can make them as the opportunity arises.

✔ **Tell stories.** Everyone likes short anecdotes. An example can often illustrate a point more vividly than dry data. But keep your stories very short and to the point.

✔ **Be prepared to ask questions.** Participants at a round-table are expected to ask questions. In fact, that feature is one of the biggest advantages of participating in a round-table. Participants in roundtables should come expecting to get answers, too. As they discuss various topics, the participants should be there as much to learn as to contribute. A roundtable's a forum for sharing ideas. And if you know who the other participants will be in advance, you can have specific questions ready to ask them.

✔ **Find appropriate openings for your questions.** The best time to ask a question about a particular topic is when that topic is under discussion. But what if you never get a chance or the topic doesn't come up? You can create your own opportunity to ask a specific question of a specific participant. Just conclude one of your comments by saying 'Well, I'd really like to hear from Mr So-And-So about how his company achieved record sales revenues.'

✔ **Recognise networking opportunities.** A roundtable provides more than an opportunity to state your ideas. This speaking format also allows you to develop valuable relationships with the other participants. You can really get to know them just by discussing issues together. And you can continue to cultivate those relationships after the roundtable has ended.

Chapter 17

Speaking Internationally

· ·

In This Chapter

▶ Finding out information about other cultures

▶ Getting your message across

▶ Delivering your message clearly

▶ Working with an interpreter effectively

· ·

*M*ost people wouldn't drive a car if they didn't know what the controls were or how to operate them because a good chance exists they'd have an accident. They'd hurt themselves, the car, and the people around them. But a lot of people will happily give a presentation or speech to an audience from a different culture without knowing anything about them. And doing so can be just as dangerous.

If you know nothing about your audience's culture, you'll be more likely to unintentionally offend, insult, or upset them. Your presentation will be a car crash waiting to happen. And you'll hurt yourself, your cause, and your audience. Unfortunately, the damage to your relationship with your audience is sometimes harder to repair than a broken car. So, consider this chapter your insurance policy to make sure your world doesn't collide with anyone else's and do irreparable damage.

Discovering the Culture of Your Audience

How do you find out about another culture? Ask a member of that culture. Most people are delighted to talk about their ethnic or national background. And if you tell them what you plan to say, they can help you omit anything potentially offensive. They can also give you a window into the mind of your audience. Then you can shape your speech in a way that your audience will enjoy and appreciate.

For example, say you're giving a talk in the United Arab Emirates. You may want to consider which references are too UK-centric and won't be understood. You may also want to learn about the culture, history, and politics of the region so that you can make some specific references to people, places, and current events that are relevant to the audience.

What if you don't have a contact who can guide you? Find someone who can. Do you know someone with a relative in the country where you'll be speaking? Do you know someone at a university or college? Many universities, business schools, and other institutions of higher learning have lecturers or staff from other countries. Do you know someone who works for a multinational corporation? Find out if they can get you in touch with someone from the country where you'll be presenting. And don't forget to ask the person who arranged your presentation to provide some help.

Don't assume you know about a culture because you know the popular stereotypes. Just watching television news or films won't give you an in-depth understanding. Find out what the culture is really like. You'll spare yourself a lot of embarrassment.

Crafting Your Message

We've provided in the following sections some important rules to keep in mind when you're preparing to present to an audience from another country or culture.

Keeping it as simple as possible

The time for brilliant rhetorical flourishes, witty turns of phrase, and complex message structures isn't when you're addressing non-native speakers of your language. Give the audience a break. Keep your sentences short and your vocabulary as simple as possible. And provide very clear transitions that let the audience know when you're moving from one point to another. (See Chapter 8 for more on transitions.)

Doing so increases the chance that you communicate rather than confuse. (Making yourself understood, however, *doesn't* mean that you should talk to your audience like they're 2-year-olds.)

Quoting someone from the audience's country or culture

Every country and culture has its heroes. Authors. Artists. Scientists. Politicians. Pick a native who is admired by your audience and quote that person in your presentation. Doing so will communicate that you went to the trouble of discovering something about your audience's culture, and this effort will be perceived favourably.

Don't just force in a quotation. Tie it into a point that you're making. Otherwise, you'll appear to be pandering to the audience.

Adapting substance and style to cultural needs

Different countries and cultures have different preferences regarding how they like presenters to behave. For example, North American audiences like speakers who are very passionate (or even over-the-top in their style of delivery) about their topic – they are also happier interacting with the speaker, for example, putting their hands up or shouting answers out to questions. Audiences in India and Sri Lanka can appear quite disinterested as they tend to shy away from any form of audience participation and at the end will applaud only gently – even if they really enjoyed and valued your presentation. Far-East Asian audiences are often less impressed by rhetoric and performance than they are by a solid argument backed up by robust data.

Keeping it as short as possible

Listening to a presentation or speech in your native language can be tiring. So try to imagine how tiring it is to listen to a speech in a non-native language. Audience fatigue is why you should keep your speech as short as possible. If you have a lot of content to deliver, consider scheduling break periods for your audience.

Using worldwide examples

Do all the examples and references in your presentation come from your own country? If so, you risk appearing pompous and arrogant when you're speaking outside your country. Find some examples from elsewhere in the world. Or at least acknowledge that such examples exist. (You just didn't have time to research them.) Implying that your country is superior to theirs doesn't win over foreign audiences.

People from the USA like to refer to themselves as Americans. As you can imagine, people from countries in Central America and South America get rightly annoyed about it. They're also Americans.

Avoiding humour

What makes something funny? Although we could write a dissertation on this subject (and many have), the short answer is that a lot of humour is rooted in cultural values. So something hilarious in one culture may not be seen as such in another. Unless you're very familiar with the culture, using humour is usually a mistake; avoid doing so unless you're sure it transcends cultural boundaries (see the nearby sidebar, 'Emergency laughs'). No one may get your joke, or even worse, they may find it offensive.

Getting rid of idioms

Every language has colloquial expressions that cause confusion if translated literally. Avoid them. Actively search for idioms in your presentation or speech and eliminate them.

Take the phrase 'born with a silver spoon in his mouth'. Most English speakers understand the saying to mean a person who was born into a rich family. But speakers of other languages may think the expression refers to a person with a unique birth defect.

Emergency laughs

We once came across a marketing executive for Hewlett-Packard who gave presentations to audiences around the world. And he always began in the same way: 'I'm glad to be here. I've only been here a few days, but I'm already picking up your language.' Then he'd say the following phrase in the language of his audience: 'A life-vest is located beneath your seat in case of emergency.'

No matter where he went, his audiences always laughed. This line was a great way to break the ice.

Everyone knows the line from the safety card on an airplane. The safety card is always written in several languages, so on the plane to wherever he was going, he'd memorise the line in the language of that country. He'd also write it down and ask colleagues from the country he was visiting to make sure he was pronouncing it correctly after he arrived at his destination.

Using humour when speaking to an audience from another culture can be risky. But this particular line works because it transcends cultural boundaries. Anyone who has ever flown in a plane gets it.

Even among English speakers, idiomatic expressions can cause confusion. Cultural commentators sometimes say that the British and North Americans are two nations *divided* by a common language. For example, what North Americans call 'pants' we call trousers.

Losing the jargon and acronyms

Jargon and acronyms are confusing enough when you're talking to native speakers of your language. These devices are even worse when you're talking to non-native speakers. If you have to use jargon, make sure you define it for the audience. And explain what each letter of your acronyms stand for. But avoid both whenever possible.

Using appropriate sports metaphors

Football is probably the most popular sport in the world, so you're fairly safe using football metaphors about scoring goals, tackling the opposition, and so on. But other sports don't always travel so well. For example, we talk about hockey, but when North Americans talk about hockey, they automatically mean *ice* hockey. If you intend to use sports metaphors, use them from sports that are popular in the country where you're presenting.

Getting the numbers right

If you're talking about money or measurements, convert your numbers into the system used by the nation where you'll be speaking. For example, many Europeans would have no idea how tall someone is if they were described as a six-foot-four giant. Remember that most of the world uses the metric system.

Being cautious about holiday references

A holiday in one country isn't necessarily a holiday in another. And some holidays have the same names but different dates and meanings. For example, Easter and Christmas are particular to Christian countries. And while every country has a fifth of May in its calendar, only Mexico celebrates Cinco de Mayo. This day is *not* a holiday for other Central American countries.

Getting graphic

Using visual aids with lots of graphic symbols when you're speaking to a foreign audience may seem like a good idea. But often graphics don't travel well. Although some symbols are used in most places around the world (for example, men's and women's toilet symbols – except in the Middle East, where men wear long garments and so do the images on the door), many are culture specific. For example, a piggy bank means savings to a British audience, but in some countries it would merely indicate a disgusting animal. And a thumbs-up image – meaning approval in some countries – is *very* offensive in others. So make sure that the graphic symbols you use mean what you think they'll mean to your audience.

Colouring with caution

A potential pitfall with visual aids is colour. The problem is that different cultures assign different symbolic meanings to colours. For example, in western cultures white is associated with purity and weddings. In Asian cultures, white is associated with death and funerals. Red symbolises rage in the UK. But red's a colour for happiness and prosperity in the Far East. So find out what colours symbolise for your audience before you make your visual aids, so you won't paint yourself into a corner.

Making magnificent handouts

Handouts are useful when you're speaking to people who aren't native speakers of your language. A written summary of your remarks will help them understand and recall more of your message – especially if the handouts are in their language. But make sure the translation is correct – and that it doesn't offend any of the cultural sensibilities of your audience. Ask someone from that culture to review your handouts before you give them out.

Watch out for the following:

- ✔ **Dates:** Use the format of the country where you'll be speaking. In Europe, 12/8/06 means 12 August 2006. In the USA, the digits for the month and day are swapped, so it means December 8 2006.

- ✔ **Phone numbers:** Don't forget to include the country code as part of any phone listing. So overseas people calling the UK may need to add +44 and to delete the first zero of your phone number. So 020 8000 1234 may become + 44 20 8000 1234. And remember that '0800' numbers that provide toll-free calls in the UK don't usually apply in other countries.

✔ **Money symbols:** The $ sign is used in connection with several different currencies. For example, do you mean Australian dollars, Hong Kong dollars, or US dollars? Indicate what country the $ refers to by adding a prefix such as AUS$, HK$, and US$, respectively.

Adapting Your Delivery

When you're presenting in the international arena, just having a carefully prepared message isn't enough to ensure success. You also have to deliver your message properly. Doing so means adapting your style to the cultural requirements of your audience. Check out some general rules to keep in mind in the following sections.

Getting there ahead of time

Not just to the room where you'll be speaking (although doing so is a good idea). Get to the country where you'll be speaking far enough ahead of time to compensate for jet lag and to adjust to the time zone.

Projecting humility

The best way to win over audiences from any culture is to project the fact that you care for them and are really interested in them. You're really happy and honoured to be presenting to them. In contrast, the opposite approach – arrogantly communicating that the audience has got lucky by being in your presence – is a big turnoff.

Talking the talk

For a speaker to address an audience that speaks a different language to start by saying a few words or a sentence in that language is almost a cliché. (Typically, the presenter says something like 'I'm happy to be here today' in whatever language is native to the audience.) This gesture shows that the speaker tried to learn a little of the audience's language.

If you're only going to learn one line, save it for the end of your presentation. If you've established a connection with the audience, ending with a line in their language really cements the relationship. You can end by saying, 'Thank you for being here with me today' in their language.

If you want to open with a line in the audience's language, learn how to say, 'I'm sorry for not knowing how to speak your language.' This line is much more effective than a greeting like, 'I'm happy to be here today.' (See the earlier section, 'Projecting humility'.)

Eating their food

If you're speaking at a lunch or dinner meeting or any other event where food is involved, you have to eat some. You can tell people of another culture that they're great, you love them, and they're wonderful. But if you don't eat their food, they won't believe you. You have to eat what your audience are eating. So unless you have a specific dietary restriction due to health or religious reasons – *bon appétit.*

Speaking slowly

Slow down. If you're not presenting to native speakers, don't speak at your normal rate. Give your audience some time to mentally translate what you're saying. (But don't slow down so much that you're insulting. You're not talking to children.) Elongating your pauses between sentences should be enough.

Interpreting reactions

Don't assume you're doing well or badly based on your own culture's typical reactions to a presenter. Other cultures can react quite differently. For example, in the UK, an audience that takes notes generally indicates that the presenter is communicating useful information and doing well. But in Japan, the audience will take notes to be polite – even if the presenter is terrible. Some cultures show approval of a presenter by applauding, others show respect by remaining silent.

Just as you should know what the audience's reactions mean in their culture, you need to know how they may interpret *your* body language. So be very careful with the body language you use in your speech. A harmless gesture in one culture can be highly offensive in another. See Chapter 12 for specific examples.

Following protocol

Outside the UK, protocol often assumes a much more important role in presentations and the speech-making process. Speakers are sometimes expected to give and receive gifts or recognise dignitaries in the audience. If you don't want to risk offending your audience, find out the traditions and rituals that they expect you to follow. The person who arranged your speaking engagement should be able to help you with this.

Working with foreign voltage

If you're planning to use visual aids such as PowerPoint, make sure that your equipment conforms to the electrical standards of the country in which you'll be presenting. This advice may sound obvious, but many speakers forget. Just go to a search engine on the Web and type 'voltage converter' plus the name of the nation where you'll be speaking. You'll find out exactly what you need to know.

Part VI
The Part of Tens

'Rather disappointing turnout for your gardening talk, Mr Littelbogg, but our local gardening club are doing their best to fill the village hall.'

In this part . . .

*H*umour can be a useful tool in public speaking, so, in this part, we show you lots of simple ways to use humour in a presentation or speech even if you can't tell a joke. And to make you feel even more secure for your next talk, we give you a list of things to check before you speak. To finish off, we provide you with our top tips for banishing any presentation anxiety you may feel.

Chapter 18

Ten Types of Humour That Anyone Can Use

*H*umour is a powerful communication tool. It can gain attention, create rapport, and make a presentation more memorable. Humour can also relieve tension, motivate an audience, and enhance your reputation if used appropriately. Can't tell a joke? Don't worry. You have lots of other options for incorporating humour into your presentation.

Using Personal Anecdotes

A personal anecdote is a story based on a real experience – yours or someone else's. It can be a story about something that happened with friends or relatives, or an incident from work, school, home, or anywhere. An anecdote is about your life. These tales provide an absolute gold mine of humorous material for any presentation or speech. And the best feature of anecdotes is – *you can tell them*. You've already been telling them for years. So you don't have to worry about delivery.

Instead of telling these stories for no particular reason while conversing with friends or acquaintances, use them for a purpose: To make a point. Use the following list to prompt your thinking and dredge your memory for interesting, silly, odd, peculiar incidents, accidents, and happenings:

✔ An embarrassing incident in which you ended up feeling a bit silly.

✔ Any accidents or incidents you had when you were learning to drive.

✔ The last strange dream you had.

✔ Any misunderstandings you ever had.

✔ Any funny habits or tics your parents or other relatives have.

✔ Silly situations you found yourself in at school or university.

✔ The trials and tribulations of unsuccessful dates and relationships.

Just about any of these situations could be turned into a funny anecdote. Especially if you're willing to laugh at yourself, you'll find that your audience will laugh with you, too.

Analogies

An analogy is a comparison between two objects or concepts. A funny analogy makes the comparison in an entertaining way. And analogies don't require comic delivery because they're so short.

You've probably seen those posters that say stuff like: 'Ten reasons why a beer is better than a woman. . .' or 'why chocolate is better than a man. . .'. For example, have you heard this one? 'Men are like a fine wine – they just need a woman to stomp the stuffing out of them until they turn into something acceptable to have dinner with.'

Now we admit that funny analogies are difficult to think up yourself, but you can use other people's analogies in your own presentations by switching some of the facts. For example, the analogy about the man and the fine wine is a perfect example. It could apply to just about any role – for example: 'A junior lawyer is just like a fine wine – they just need a partner to stomp the stuffing out of them until they turn into something acceptable to have dinner with.' So, anytime you come across a funny analogy, write it down and file it away. You can never have too many at your fingertips.

Quotes

Funny quotes provide an easy way to get attention. Call this phenomenon the cult of celebrity. Call it a fascination with the quoteworthy. Whatever you want to call it, the power of the quote remains the same – as soon as an audience hears a famous name, it perks up. If the famous name is followed by a really funny quote, then you've got them. (At least for a few seconds, anyway.)

Here's a handful of random quotes. With a little creative thinking, you may be able to integrate them into your presentations:

- ✔ 'Committee – a group of men who keep minutes and waste hours.' M. Berle

- ✔ 'I spent 90 per cent of my money on women and drink. The rest I wasted.' George Best

- ✔ 'I have nothing to declare except my genius.' Oscar Wilde

- ✔ 'I am free of all prejudices. I hate everyone equally.' W. C. Fields.

Cartoons

Even people who insist that they can't tell a joke admit that they can describe a cartoon that appeared in a newspaper or magazine. You probably see people do this all the time. You join a gathering of colleagues taking a coffee break. The conversation turns to some business topic, and the person describes a cartoon from a newspaper that relates to the discussion. Everyone laughs, and the conversation continues. If you can do this (and we know you can), you can use cartoons to make points in a presentation or speech.

Of course, one of the best ways to use a cartoon is to show it on a big screen. You should get permission to use it first, but a cartoon almost always generates a chuckle amongst your audience – especially if you use a well-known character such as *Posy* or *Snoopy* and *Charlie Brown* from the *Peanuts* comic strip.

Definitions

Funny definitions are extremely easy to use. Just pick a word or phrase from your presentation and define it in an amusing way.

Try using a dictionary for inserting funny definitions into your talk. Pick out a word or phrase that you look up in the dictionary and then state the meaning. Here are a few examples that you may be able to incorporate into a variety of different presentations and talks:

- ✔ An adult: A person who has stopped growing at both ends and is now growing in the middle.

- ✔ Boss: Someone who is early when you are late and late when you are early.

- ✔ Diplomat: A person who tells you to go to hell in such a way that you actually look forward to the trip.

- ✔ Log on: What you say when you want to make the fire hotter.

- ✔ Politician: Someone who shakes your hand before elections and your confidence after.

- ✔ Myth: A female moth.

Where do you find funny definitions? Most 'treasury of funny stuff for public speakers' books contain them. Just look in your local library or a large book shop. Trade journals and professional magazines are also good sources. These types of publications often have a humour page that includes amusing definitions related to their readers' occupations. The Web can also provide you with lots of free information – just try typing into a search engine such as www.google.co.uk the word 'humour' along with the topic you are trying to liven up, such as 'lawyer', 'parent', or 'environment'.

Abbreviations and Acronyms

An abbreviation is formed by combining the first letters of a series of words. Two familiar (but boring) examples are VAT (Value Added Tax) and the accounting principle known as LIFO (Last In First Out). Funny abbreviations are much more entertaining.

You can make abbreviations funny in a variety of ways. The simplest way is to change the meaning of the underlying words. For example, we all know that the BBC is the British Broadcasting Corporation, but with the advent of all this reality television, you may suggest to an audience that they could change their name to stand for the Big Brother Corporation.

Acronyms (abbreviations that form a word) can also be used in a humorous way. You can make up amusing acronyms by abbreviating a funny phrase. Say you're talking about corporate social responsibility: 'Ten or 15 years ago, corporate social responsibility was a MEGO topic . . . My Eyes Glaze Over . . . but not today.'

Here are some other amusing examples:

- ✔ CRAFT: Can't Remember a Flipping Thing
- ✔ DNA: Do Not Ask
- ✔ MELVIN: Mediocrity, Ego, Limits, Vanity, Incompetent, Name-calling
- ✔ MUPET: Most Useless Person Ever Trained

Signs

Have you ever seen a sign that made you laugh? They're all over the place these days. The 'You Want It When?' sign on a secretary's wall. The 'Mistakes Made While You Wait' sign hanging by a bank cashier's window. The 'Your Failure to Plan Does Not Constitute an Emergency on Our Part' sign taped to the wall of a print shop. All of these are potential material for a presentation. You just describe the sign and where you saw it. Then tie it to a point.

Laws

We live in a world of laws – civil, criminal, and scientific. But no matter where we live, all of us answer to a higher law – Murphy's. Murphy's law famously states that anything that can go wrong, will go wrong. This 'mother of all laws' has spawned quite a brood. You can find entire books of Murphy-style laws, so you can probably find a law that fits your subject matter. Why bother? Because funny laws provide a simple way to add humour to a presentation.

Here are some examples of bizarre laws that you could try to slot into your presentation:

- ✔ On the island of Jersey, it's against the law for a man to knit during the fishing season.

- ✔ It is illegal to sell an ET doll in France. They have a law forbidding the sale of dolls that do not have human faces.

- ✔ In Alabama, USA, it is illegal for a driver to be blindfolded while operating a vehicle.

Some of these laws may have since been repealed or are entirely fictitious to begin with. This isn't a law textbook – so please don't hold us accountable.

Greeting Cards

Would you like free access to easy-to-deliver material developed by highly paid humour writers? Then walk into your local card shop and start browsing. Birthday cards. Anniversary cards. Get well cards. You name it. What was once a field devoted to solemn sentiments is now dominated by mirthful messages. And you can adapt them easily to almost anything that you want to speak about.

Bumper Stickers

One of the great breakthroughs in the history of presentations and public speaking occurred with the invention of the car. The car provided a fantastic new source of material – bumper stickers.

From stickers concerning driving ('Forget world peace – visualise using your indicator') to stickers offering self-insight ('I just got lost in thought. It was unfamiliar territory') and general advice ('Be nice to your kids. They'll choose your nursing home'), wisdom previously limited to great minds became available to the masses.

Here's one we saw that may relate to change (whether in your work, your home, or your life in general:

'Change is good. You go first.'

And if you don't want to look for bumper stickers, you can also find funny lines on t-shirts, coffee mugs, and just about any other object that has a printable surface.

So there you have it. A chapter of help for the humour-impaired. If you can't tell a joke, you can still tell a personal anecdote, make an amusing observation, quote a funny line, or employ many other simple types of humour. Any of them can enhance your next presentation or speech.

Chapter 19

Ten Things to Check Before You Give a Presentation

. . . .

In This Chapter

▶ Arranging the room to your benefit

▶ Anticipating equipment problems

▶ Eliminating distractions

. . . .

*Y*ou prepare a fantastic presentation. You run it by your colleagues. Everyone says the content's pure genius. Can't miss. You're going to be great. The big day arrives and you're feeling good. You take your incredibly clever PowerPoint slides and go to the site of your presentation. The audience applauds as you enter the room. But you wish you were dead. The podium you requested isn't there. Neither is the microphone or the projector. And the way the room is set-up, half your audience couldn't even see your PowerPoint visuals anyway.

Rather than being stuck on stage without the right equipment, maximise your chances of giving a successful presentation by taking care of the following *before* you start talking.

Sound System

Is there a sound system and does it work? Make sure that the volume is adjusted so that everyone in the room can hear you. *Test the microphone in the location where you'll actually use it.* Microphones often work effectively in some parts of the room but not in others. For example, if the microphone is too close to some of the equipment, it may generate deafening, screeching feedback. Or if the equipment's too far away, the microphone lead may not stretch to where you need to stand. Or if you're using a wireless microphone, the signal may not be strong enough. So make sure you test the microphone where you'll be standing and moving.

In testing the volume level, don't just say the usual 'testing, testing, one, two, three' – unless those words are part of your actual presentation. Try saying the first few sentences of your presentation in your normal speaking voice and ask someone to move to different parts of the room or auditorium to make sure you can be heard clearly.

And make sure that you know how to work the microphone. Do you know how to turn it on and off? If you have a microphone stand, do you know how to adjust its height or angle? Different microphones pick up and broadcast your voice in different ways. Play with the microphone until you get a good idea of its range.

Podium

Is a podium or lectern provided? And is it the right size? The *right size* is whatever suits your purpose. Do you want the audience to see you? Then make sure you're taller than the podium or that you get a box you can stand on behind it. Are you afraid the audience will throw things? Get a high – and wide – podium. In either case, make sure that the podium has a light and that it works – especially if you're going to darken the room for overhead transparencies. You can't get the audience to see the light if the podium leaves your notes in the dark.

Audiovisual Equipment

You can't check overhead or PowerPoint projectors too many times. After you get your overhead transparencies or PowerPoint slides focused, walk around the room while one is projecting on the screen. Can it be seen from everywhere in the room? Projectors often block the view of people seated in line with them. If some of the audience's view is obscured, try to project your overhead or slide higher up on the screen – closer to the ceiling. And definitely use a screen. A screen shows your overheads or slides much more clearly than a wall. Many projectors come equipped with a spare bulb. Make sure you know where it is.

If your visuals are in PowerPoint, make sure you'll have a computer available with the PowerPoint software, and a way to get your presentation material onto it (or, better yet, bring your own laptop). Make sure the right cables are with the projector (power for the projector and the right connector cable for the computer). If you're using video or DVD, be certain the right equipment to show it is available, and that it can easily be seen and heard by all members of the audience.

Lighting

Test the 'house lights' to see if they work and how the light fills the room. Find out if you can adjust their level of brightness. If the lights are adjustable, take advantage of this feature – especially if you're using overheads or PowerPoint.

Although overheads require that you turn the lights off, if they're easy to see, you can show them with the lights turned down but *not* off. A small amount of light makes a tremendous difference in your interaction with the audience. They can't go to sleep under the cover of darkness.

Human Equipment

If people are operating equipment for you, make sure that they know what they're doing. You don't need an Einstein to work an overhead projector, but a minimal level of competence is required. And you need to tell them what verbal or nonverbal cues (for example, a nod of the head or hand gesture) you'll use to indicate you're ready for the next transparency. Also, make sure that you know who to contact for help with minor and major catastrophes – a light bulb burns out, a microphone breaks, or your podium is destroyed by a UFO.

Electricity and Water

Where are the electrical sockets in the room? Do you have enough of them to run your equipment? Are they two-prong or three-prong (if you're presenting elsewhere in Europe, for example)? Do yourself a favour. Always bring an adapter and an extension lead (and perhaps a 6- or 8-way extension lead in case the room has only one socket but you have multiple items to plug in).

A lot of presenters get a dry throat from projecting their voice to an audience. So make sure you have a bottle of water to hand if you need it. You don't want to lose your voice or get gradually quieter and quieter as your throat gets drier and drier.

Toilets

Definitely check the toilets. Where are they located? Do they have paper towels available? Is there an adequate supply of toilet paper? If in doubt, take some toilet paper with you! Do the toilets work? These details may sound trivial now, but they can become very important. You never know when you'll need a toilet in a hurry – especially if you're nervous.

Seating Arrangements

For seating, three basic considerations apply to any type of speech in any type of setting:

- ✔ First and most important, can everyone see you?
- ✔ Is the seating comfortable – both physically and psychologically?
- ✔ Is the arrangement of chairs suited to the size of the room, the size of the audience, and the purpose of your presentation?

In considering these seating factors, start with the room. Will you be in a banquet room? A conference room? A large meeting room? An auditorium? The room establishes the parameters for seating. Next, will the audience be seated at tables? If so, will the tables be round or rectangular? After you have this information, you can arrange the seating pieces like a jigsaw puzzle until you get the picture that you want.

Within the boundaries established by the room and furniture, you can arrange seating based on the size of the room and your purpose. Chairs arranged in a semicircle provide a more informal atmosphere. This arrangement puts you directly in front of each audience member. A semicircle also allows all the audience members to see each other. If the audience consists of more than 30 people, the group is probably too large for a single semicircle. In that case, you can stagger a second row of chairs behind the first row. Now you have a double semicircle where the second row looks between the shoulders of the people in the first row. For large groups or a more formal atmosphere, we recommend classroom-style seating in rows.

If you're presenting at a breakfast, lunch, or dinner meeting, the audience will probably be seated at round tables, which means that half of them will have their backs to you when you begin to speak. Factor this detail in when you begin your speech or presentation. Leave time for people to turn their seats around to face you.

Potential Distractions

If you're presenting at a restaurant, hotel, or office building, chances are a nice view can be seen through the window of the meeting room.

An attractive view's bad news, because you want audience attention focused on you, not the view. What can you do? First, try to speak in a room that has no windows. If that situation's not possible, make sure that the windows are covered with blinds or curtains. What if they have no curtains? Well, if the view is spectacular and you need to get rid of the distraction – improvise. We've seen speakers hang tablecloths over the windows – anything to eliminate the competition of the view.

Noise is another big distraction. Background babble provides direct competition with your message. If you're presenting at a grazing function – a breakfast, lunch, or dinner – don't start your talk until the waiters have cleared the tables. The clatter of dishes is an intolerable distraction. Unfortunately, due to 'time problems', your contact may insist that you begin speaking before the meal is concluded. Try this tactic. Suggest that the waiters serve dessert and disappear. They can clear the dessert plates *after* you finish your presentation or speech. You start talking as soon as the waiters leave the room. The noise of people eating dessert while you're speaking is a drag, but that situation's a lot better than trying to talk with waiters running around the room.

How to Get There

Do you know exactly where you're giving your presentation, how to get there, and how long it takes to get there? Well, find out. You'd be amazed how little consideration people give to these basic concerns. You knock yourself out preparing a killer presentation, and then you blow it by going to the wrong ballroom. Knowing the hotel isn't enough. You need to know the *exact* location. Why? Because by the time you get to the correct room, you're frazzled and possibly even late. The time you were going to spend getting used to the room and gearing yourself up is gone forever.

Related concerns are traffic and parking. Don't plan your timetable on some general notion of how long it takes to get to the meeting site. Plan specifically for the time you'll be travelling. Maybe the journey generally takes 30 minutes. If you have to travel during rush hour, the journey's going to take longer. Plan for it.

Then you have the whole parking thing. You need to know in advance where to park. Hey, you're the speaker. Tell your contact to give you a special parking spot at the meeting site. You deserve it.

Chapter 20

Ten Ways to Overcome the Fear Factor

. . . .

In This Chapter

▶ Handling the symptoms of nervousness

▶ Using psychological techniques to banish stress

▶ Focusing the audience's attention away from yourself

. . . .

*W*e all get nervous. In fact, very few people exist who don't feel some hint of nervousness when they have to stand up in front of an audience. A lot of the professional speakers we know still say that they experience a touch of stage fright just before they get onto the stage – even if they've spoken hundreds of times and to thousands and thousands of people.

The good news is that you can take plenty of steps to ensure that nervousness doesn't ruin your presentation. In fact, with a little bit of effort, you can use these techniques and tricks to deliver a pretty outstanding presentation. In this chapter, we share our top ten tips for dealing with that fear factor.

Getting It in Perspective

A colleague once got very upset and nervous before a meeting. She was worried about having to give a presentation to a client organisation. She was pacing around the office, fidgeting, and kept asking other colleagues, 'What am I going to do? What if it doesn't go well?'

One of our colleagues sat her down, took hold of both her hands, looked her in the eyes, and said, 'What's the worst that could happen – is anyone going to die?'

Sometimes we can worry too much about a situation – especially nerve-wracking circumstances such as presenting in front of an audience – if we think about it too much and we let the problem get bigger and bigger in our heads.

So ask yourself these questions whenever you start to feel that mounting panic:

- ✔ Will your presentation kill anyone?
- ✔ Will they take your children away as a result of a bad presentation?
- ✔ Will your company go bankrupt as a result of a bad presentation?

The very act of measuring an event's impact on our lives can often have a very tangible effect in putting things into perspective and managing some of that fear factor.

Breathing Right

Psychologists have discovered that our minds and bodies are inextricably linked. Using a physical technique called *diaphragmatic breathing* can help you feel more mentally confident.

Practise diaphragmatic breathing at home by working through the following steps:

1. **Begin by lying down on a completely flat but fairly unyielding surface.** If your bed or sofa is very soft, then try lying on the carpet or a blanket on the floor.

2. **Place your right hand on your chest and your left hand on your belly button.**

3. **Now breathe only into your chest area.** Only your chest should rise and fall – that is, your right hand will move, but your left hand should stay still. These three steps will give you the chance to experience shallow

breathing – the kind of breaths we tend to take when we're nervous or angry. If you continue to breathe into your chest, you may feel dizzy and uncomfortable.

4. **Now take slow deep breaths into your belly.** Only your left hand should rise and fall; your right hand should stay completely still. Inhale to a count of four, and exhale to a count of four. After you get into the method of diaphragmatic breathing, you should feel very relaxed.

 Keep practising diaphragmatic breathing at home. Eventually, if you engage in this technique just before you need to give a presentation, you should be able to summon up that feeling of relaxation anywhere and at any time and banish those nerves.

Handling Bodily Symptoms of Stress

When we get nervous, our bodies tense up. So make an effort to relax the tension in your muscles in order to also release the tension in your head.

When you start to feel nervous, try to systematically relax all of the muscles in your body, starting from your head and working through to your toes:

1. **Clench your jaw and screw up all the muscles in your face.** Hold for a count of three and release. When you release, you'll feel blood rushing back into your facial muscles – warm, lovely blood carrying oxygen and nutrients back to your facial muscles to relax them.

2. **Repeat with your neck and shoulders** – lift your shoulders and bunch up the muscles in your neck for a few seconds before you relax them. Then perform a few small circular movements with your shoulders to make sure the muscles are not bunched up any more.

3. **Clench your fists together as hard as you can.** Hold for a count of three and then release. Wiggle your fingers to ensure they're not tense.

4. **Tighten your biceps (imagine that you're a body builder) and squeeze those muscles together for a count of three.** Then release.

5. **Clench your buttock muscles for a count of three and release.**

6. **Sit down, and clench your toes together for a count of three.** Release, wiggle them, and feel the muscular tension eddy away from your body.

Challenging Negative Thoughts

When we get nervous, we experience *automatic negative thoughts* such as, 'Oh no, it's all going to go horribly wrong', 'I can't do this', or 'I wish I could curl up and hide'. These uncensored views pop into our head whenever we feel nervous. Having these dark thoughts occasionally isn't wrong, but letting them dominate our thoughts can derail our confidence.

Begin to identify and challenge negative thoughts that pop into your head. Whenever you hear one of these unhelpful thoughts in your own head, then challenge it. Begin by acknowledging that you're experiencing a negative automatic thought. If you hear your inner voice make a negative claim about you or your presentation, then say to yourself 'That's an automatic negative thought'. Remind yourself, 'That's my unconscious talking – that's not the "real" me.'

You can also make sure that negative thoughts don't derail your performance by replacing them with positive thoughts. Just as negative thoughts can trigger negative emotions, positive thoughts can trigger relaxed, confident moods.

Positive affirmations are constructive statements about yourself. Long before you need to give your presentation, prepare a set of statements that you can repeat to yourself, such as: 'I am confident, I have done my research, and I know my material' or 'I am confident, I am smiley, and happy'. Then repeat your positive affirmations when you start to feel nervous. But don't just repeat them in a half-hearted way. Find somewhere quiet where you can say them out loud as if you mean them!

To be effective, positive affirmations should always be phrased in terms of what you want ('I am calm and centred') rather than what you want to avoid ('I am not nervous').

Visualising Success

Top sports people use visualisation techniques all the time to perform at their very best. So why not use this great method for evicting those feelings of nervousness? If you can picture in your mind how it would look for you to succeed, your brain will send nerve impulses to release chemicals into your bloodstream that promote positive emotions.

When you're preparing for that presentation, practise visualising how you would like it to go. It doesn't matter if you don't know what the room looks like or where the audience will be seated. You're only imagining how your performance will look.

Find a quiet place and picture yourself giving the presentation. Imagine yourself smiling and being warm and confident. Imagine the gestures you will make and the bits of your presentation that you will punctuate. Picture the audience laughing at your jokes, applauding at the appropriate moments, and then giving you a rapturous send-off at the conclusion of your talk. The more times you visualise what success will look like, the more likely it is that you'll actually succeed.

Faking It Until You Can Make It

You can feel a touch of nerves. But the important thing is not to show it. Fake being calm and confident for long enough, and you'll soon feel calm and confident.

Make sure that you don't fall prey to any of the common signs of nerves:

- ✓ **Fidgeting:** Touching your hair repeatedly or scratching your nose are common signs that you don't feel as comfortable as you seem. So make sure you control your fidgeting.

- ✓ **Pacing:** By all means walk around the stage to make your presentation visually more interesting than just standing on one spot. But don't throw yourself around the stage too much. Pacing excessively is another big give-away that you aren't as confident as you should be.

✔ **Sweating:** Dress appropriately for the big day. If you have a tendency to sweat through your clothing, think about wearing dark colours or keeping your jacket on for the presentation itself.

✔ **Shaky hands:** Try to keep your hands in a neutral position (clasped lightly in front of your body or steepled – Chapter 12 shows you how to do this). And put any notes down on a lectern or podium so the audience can't see your sheets of paper shaking.

Practising, Practising, Practising

Practice makes perfect. Practice makes perfect. Practice makes perfect. What does practice make?

The more you practise, the more you'll get to know your material. You'll need to consult your notes less. You can concentrate on making eye contact with your audience. The benefits of practising properly are very concrete.

When you practise, try to simulate the real presentation conditions as closely as possible. Rehearse your speech out loud and at the right volume. If you'll be standing up when you give your presentation, stand up when you practise. If you can, project your slides up onto a flat surface and practise gesturing at your slides, too.

We know of top presenters who practise their talks all the way through, from start to finish, up to a dozen or more times in order to get their presentations word-perfect. If you want to be good, then practise. If you want to be great, practise a lot.

Becoming Familiar with the Environment

The last thing you need is to get up in front of your audience to find that your microphone doesn't work or the light in the overhead projector has blown.

Work through this checklist of questions to make sure that you are comfortable with your environment, including the props:

- ✔ Do you know where the toilets are?

- ✔ Does the sound system work?

- ✔ Can you operate the overhead projector/PowerPoint slides?

- ✔ Have you got a glass of water in case your throat goes dry?

- ✔ (If you need to) do you know how to dim the lights for your presentation?

- ✔ Do you know where you'll be sitting before your presentation? And do you know where you'll need to return to after it?

Diverting the Audience's Attention

Standing up in front of an audience can be especially nerve-wracking if all eyes are on you. But all eyes don't have to be on you. In fact, you may be able to divert all attention away from yourself for at least part of your presentation.

Visual aids are a great way to get the audience focusing their attention on something other than you. If you have a slide with just three lines of text on screen at any one time, the audience is going to be looking at you more than if, say, you display a slide with six lines of text.

If you want to get the audience looking entirely away from you for a part of your presentation, why not include a short video clip in your presentation? You could use that time – whether it's 30 seconds, a minute or 5 minutes – to catch your breath, maybe look through your notes, and gather your thoughts for the next part of your presentation.

Using Whatever Works for You

Everyone has different stress-busting techniques. No list is ever going to be comprehensive. So think about the techniquess you use to calm yourself down in other situations.

Tricks that we've heard people use include:

- ✔ Using emotional anchors that remind them of when they feel relaxed – such as taking a 'lucky' keepsake along with them.
- ✔ Running their wrists under a cold tap in order to cool their body temperature down and wash away tension.
- ✔ Praying.
- ✔ Planting friendly people in the audience that they can make eye contact with.
- ✔ Using aromatherapy candles or fragrances to promote relaxation.

Why not have a think about what else might work for you?

Index

FOR DUMMIES

Do Anything. Just Add Dummies

HOME

UK editions

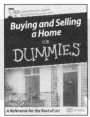

Buying and Selling a Home

0-7645-7027-7

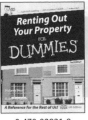

Renting Out Your Property

0-470-02921-8

DIY & Home Maintenance

0-7645-7054-4

PERSONAL FINANCE

Investing

0-7645-7023-4

Paying Less Tax 2006/2007

0-470-02860-2

Sorting Out Your Finances

0-7645-7039-0

BUSINESS

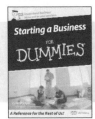

Starting a Business

0-7645-7018-8

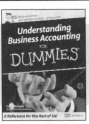

Understanding Business Accounting

0-7645-7025-0

Business Plans

0-7645-7026-9

British History For Dummies
(0-470-03536-6)

Buying a Property in Eastern Europe For Dummies
(0-7645-7047-1)

Cognitive Behavioural Therapy For Dummies
(0-470-01838-0)

Cricket For Dummies
(0-470-03454-8)

Diabetes For Dummies
(0-7645-7019-6)

Detox For Dummies
(0-470-01908-5)

eBay.co.uk For Dummies
(0-7645-7059-5)

Genealogy Online For Dummies
(0-7645-7061-7)

Life Coaching For Dummies
(0-470-03135-2)

Neuro-linguistic Programming For Dummies
(0-7645-7028-5)

Parenting For Dummies
(0-470-02714-2)

Rugby Union For Dummies
(0-470-03537-4)

Self Build and Renovation For Dummies
(0-470-02586-7)

Thyroid For Dummies
(0-470-03172-7)

9154_p1

Available wherever books are sold. For more information or to order direct go to www.wileyeurope.com or call 0800 243407 (Non UK call +44 1243 843296)

FOR DUMMIES®

A world of resources to help you grow

HOBBIES

Poker
FOR DUMMIES
A Reference for the Rest of Us!
0-7645-5232-5

Sewing
FOR DUMMIES
A Reference for the Rest of Us!
0-7645-6847-7

Drawing
FOR DUMMIES
A Reference for the Rest of Us!
0-7645-5476-X

Also available:

Art For Dummies
(0-7645-5104-3)

Aromatherapy
For Dummies
(0-7645-5171-X)

Bridge For Dummies
(0-7645-5015-2)

Card Games
For Dummies
(0-7645-9910-0)

Chess For Dummies
(0-7645-5003-9)

Crocheting
For Dummies
(0-7645-4151-X)

Improving Your
Memory For Dummies
(0-7645-5435-2)

Meditation
For Dummies
(0-471-77774-9)

Photography
For Dummies
(0-7645-4116-1)

Quilting For Dummies
(0-7645-9799-X)

Woodworking
For Dummies
(0-7645-3977-9)

EDUCATION

Cooking Basics
FOR DUMMIES
A Reference for the Rest of Us!
0-7645-7206-7

The Koran
FOR DUMMIES
A Reference for the Rest of Us!
0-7645-5581-2

Anatomy
& Physiology
FOR DUMMIES
A Reference for the Rest of Us!
0-7645-5422-0

Also available:

Algebra For Dummies
(0-7645-5325-9)

Astronomy For
Dummies
(0-7645-8465-0)

Buddhism For
Dummies
(0-7645-5359-3)

Calculus For Dummies
(0-7645-2498-4)

Christianity For
Dummies
(0-7645-4482-9)

Forensics For
Dummies
(0-7645-5580-4)

Islam For Dummies
(0-7645-5503-0)

Philosophy For
Dummies
(0-7645-5153-1)

Religion For Dummies
(0-7645-5264-3)

Trigonometry For
Dummies
(0-7645-6903-1)

PETS

Puppies
FOR DUMMIES
A Reference for the Rest of Us!
0-7645-5255-4

Dog Training
FOR DUMMIES
A Reference for the Rest of Us!
0-7645-8418-9

Cats
FOR DUMMIES
A Reference for the Rest of Us!
0-7645-5275-9

Also available:

Labrador Retrievers
For Dummies
(0-7645-5281-3)

Aquariums For
Dummies
(0-7645-5156-6)

Birds For Dummies
(0-7645-5139-6)

Dogs For Dummies
(0-7645-5274-0)

Ferrets For Dummies
(0-7645-5259-7)

German Shepherds
For Dummies
(0-7645-5280-5)

Golden Retrievers
For Dummies
(0-7645-5267-8)

Horses For Dummies
(0-7645-9797-3)

Jack Russell Terriers
For Dummies
(0-7645-5268-6)

9154_p2

**Available wherever books are sold. For more information or to order direct go to
www.wileyeurope.com or call 0800 243407 (Non UK call +44 1243 843296)**

FOR DUMMIES®

The easy way to get more done and have more fun

LANGUAGES

Spanish
0-7645-5194-9

French
0-7645-5193-0

Italian
0-7645-5196-5

Also available:

French Phrases
For Dummies
(0-7645-7202-4)

German
For Dummies
(0-7645-5195-7)

Hebrew For Dummies
(0-7645-5489-1)

Italian Phrases
For Dummies
(0-7645-7203-2)

Japanese
For Dummies
(0-7645-5429-8)

Latin For Dummies
(0-7645-5431-X)

Spanish Phrases
For Dummies
(0-7645-7204-0)

Spanish Verbs
For Dummies
(0-471-76872-3)

MUSIC AND FILM

Guitar
0-7645-9904-6

Filmmaking
0-7645-2476-3

Piano
0-7645-5105-1

Also available:

Bass Guitar
For Dummies
(0-7645-2487-9)

Blues For Dummies
(0-7645-5080-2)

Classical Music
For Dummies
(0-7645-5009-8)

Drums For Dummies
(0-7645-5357-7)

Jazz For Dummies
(0-471-76844-8)

Rock Guitar
For Dummies
(0-7645-5356-9)

Screenwriting
For Dummies
(0-7645-5486-7)

Songwriting
For Dummies
(0-7645-5404-2)

Singing For Dummies
(0-7645-2475-5)

HEALTH, SPORTS & FITNESS

Fitness
0-7645-7851-0

Exercise Balls
0-7645-5623-1

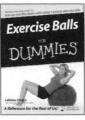

Asthma
0-7645-4233-8

Also available:

Controlling
Cholesterol
For Dummies
(0-7645-5440-9)

Dieting For Dummies
(0-7645-4149-8)

High Blood Pressure
For Dummies
(0-7645-5424-7)

Martial Arts For
Dummies
(0-7645-5358-5)

Menopause
For Dummies
(0-7645-5458-1)

Power Yoga
For Dummies
(0-7645-5342-9)

Weight Training
For Dummies
(0-471-76845-6)

Yoga For Dummies
(0-7645-5117-5)

9154_p3

**Available wherever books are sold. For more information or to order direct go to
www.wileyeurope.com or call 0800 243407 (Non UK call +44 1243 843296)**

FOR
DUMMIES®

Helping you expand your horizons and achieve your potential

INTERNET

0-7645-8996-2

0-7645-8334-4

0-7645-7327-6

Also available:

eBay.co.uk
For Dummies
(0-7645-7059-5)

Dreamweaver 8
For Dummies
(0-7645-9649-7)

Web Design
For Dummies
(0-471-78117-7)

Everyday Internet
All-in-One Desk
Reference
For Dummies
(0-7645-8875-3)

Creating Web Pages
All-in-One Desk
Reference
For Dummies
(0-7645-4345-8)

DIGITAL MEDIA

0-7645-9802-3

0-471-74739-4

0-7645-9803-1

Also available:

Digital Photos,
Movies, & Music
GigaBook
For Dummies
(0-7645-7414-0)

Photoshop CS2
For Dummies
(0-7645-9571-7)

Podcasting
For Dummies
(0-471-74898-6)

Blogging
For Dummies
(0-471-77084-1)

Digital Photography
All-in-One Desk
Reference For
Dummies
(0-7645-7328-4)

Windows XP Digital
Music For Dummies
(0-7645-7599-6)

COMPUTER BASICS

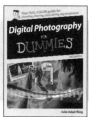

0-7645-8958-X

0-7645-7555-4

0-7645-7326-8

Also available:

Office XP 9 in 1
Desk Reference
For Dummies
(0-7645-0819-9)

PCs All-in-One Desk
Reference
For Dummies
(0-471-77082-5)

Pocket PC For
Dummies
(0-7645-1640-X)

Upgrading & Fixing
PCs For Dummies
(0-7645-1665-5)

Windows XP All-in-
One Desk Reference
For Dummies
(0-7645-7463-9)

Macs For Dummies
(0-7645-5656-8)

8322_p4

**Available wherever books are sold. For more information or to order direct go to
www.wileyeurope.com or call 0800 243407 (Non UK call +44 1243 843296)**